NORWAY
in Pictures

Eric Braun

Lerner Publications Company

Contents

Website address: www.lernerbooks.com

Lerner Publications Company
A division of Lerner Publishing Group
241 First Avenue North
Minneapolis, MN 55401 U.S.A.

web enhanced @ www.vgsbooks.com

Library of Congress Cataloging-in-Publication Data

Braun, Eric.
   Norway in pictures / by Eric Braun.—Rev. and expanded.
     p. cm. — (Visual geography series)
   Summary: An introduction to Norway, discussing its history, government, economy, people, and
culture.
   ISBN: 0-8225-0369-7 (lib. bdg. : alk. paper)
   1. Norway—Pictorial works—Juvenile literature. [1. Norway.] I. Title. II. Series.
DL413 .B73 2003
948.1—dc21   2001006614

8-9Manufactured in the United States of America
1 2 3 4 5 6 - JR - 08 07 06 05 04 03

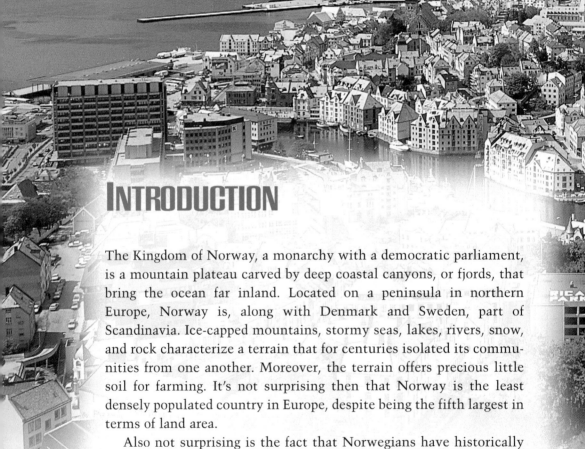

INTRODUCTION

The Kingdom of Norway, a monarchy with a democratic parliament, is a mountain plateau carved by deep coastal canyons, or fjords, that bring the ocean far inland. Located on a peninsula in northern Europe, Norway is, along with Denmark and Sweden, part of Scandinavia. Ice-capped mountains, stormy seas, lakes, rivers, snow, and rock characterize a terrain that for centuries isolated its communities from one another. Moreover, the terrain offers precious little soil for farming. It's not surprising then that Norway is the least densely populated country in Europe, despite being the fifth largest in terms of land area.

Also not surprising is the fact that Norwegians have historically been great anglers and sailors. Norwegians began to explore the North Atlantic Ocean in about A.D. 800. These were the legendary Vikings, who discovered Iceland, Greenland, and the coast of North America—the so-called New World—long before other Europeans did. Eventually, however, Norway came under the control of its

neighbors. It was ruled by the Danes for more than four centuries and by the Swedes for one. In 1905 Norway emerged as an independent nation.

After gaining self-rule, Norway quickly expanded its industries and focused on social welfare. By the mid-twentieth century, Norway had many government programs to ensure equality and a high standard of living for all Norwegians. Norwegians believe that everyone needs help at one time or another. They believe that no one should be too rich or too poor. The role of government is to make sure that every member of society receives equal treatment and prosperity. Even the royal family of Norway tries to present itself as down-to-earth in every way.

The discovery of offshore oil in 1969 allowed Norway to increase social programs and to raise the standard of living for all Norwegians. Over the past three decades, however, oil prices have proved unreliable. Also, immigration has increased, as more and more people want to make better lives for themselves through the benefits offered by this beautiful, peaceful, socially advanced country. Consequently, taxes rose while services declined at the close of the twentieth century, and dissatisfied voters forced a change of government several times.

Some people suggest that the Norwegians' strongly held belief in social welfare stems from the difficulty of life in a hostile climate and the need it creates for people to help each other survive. Indeed, Norway's land and climate contribute much to the Norwegian personality. Most Norwegians love the out-of-doors, and many of their winter athletes are revered as national icons. In addition to social equality, the government's goal has always been self-sufficiency. In spite of its limited farmland, Norway's agriculture provides more than half the country's food. Voters have twice rejected membership in the European Union (EU), a trade organization that integrates much of the rest of Europe. However, as Norway tries to build an economy that is less dependent on petroleum, it faces the possibility of losing some of its autonomy.

Many Norwegians enjoy hiking on **Jostedalsbreen,** Europe's largest glacier outside of Iceland. The rugged glacier covers 188 square miles (487 square kilometers).

Norway

— International border
-·-·- County boundary

Key to Counties
(Shown by number, near Oslo Fjord)
1. VESTFOLD
2. OSLO
3. AKERSHUS
4. ØSTFOLD

⊛ Capital city
• City

0   200 Miles
0   200 KM

N

BARENTS SEA
[ARCTIC OCEAN]

North Cape
MAGERØYA ISLAND
• Honningsvåg
• Hammerfest
• Kirkenes
FINNMARK
Tana R.
Altaelva R.
• Karasjok
RUSSIA
• Tromsø
TROMS
VESTERÅLEN ARCHIPELAGO
LOFOTEN ARCHIPELAGO
• Narvik
• Henningsvaer
MOSKENESØYA ISLAND
Maelstrom Current
• Bodø   • Fauske
NORDLAND
Arctic Circle

NORWEGIAN SEA
[NORTH ATLANTIC OCEAN]

Atlantic Current

• Mo

Vamsen R.

NORD-TRØNDELAG

Trondheim Fjord
• Stiklestad
North

Orkla River

• Trondheim
SØR-TRØNDELAG

SWEDEN

FINLAND

• Ålesund
MØRE OG ROMSDAL
• Røros

HEDMARK

SOGN OG FJORDANE
OPPLAND

Glåma River

Troll Oil Field
Sogne Fjord
• Hermansverk
• Lillehammer
Lake Mjøsa

HORDALAND
• Hol
Låden River
BUSKERUD
• Bergen
• Eidsvoll
2 3

Hardanger Fjord
⊛ Oslo
• Drammen

Bokn Fjord
• Haugesund
TELEMARK
1
4
• Skjeberg
Otra River
• Skien
• Fredrikstad
• Stavanger
ROGALAND
• Sandefjord
Oslo Fjord
VEST-AGDER
AUST-AGDER
• Kristiansand

BALTIC SEA

Ekofisk Oil Field
Skagerrak

NORTH SEA

DENMARK

THE LAND

A long, narrow, and rugged nation, Norway lies on the western edge of Europe and covers the western and northern part of the Scandinavian peninsula. The country has an area of 125,050 square miles (323,880 square kilometers), which is about the same size as the American state of New Mexico. Norway also claims overseas territories. These include Svalbard—an island group in the Arctic Ocean—and Jan Mayen, a volcanic island northeast of Iceland. Bouvet Island, which is located in the South Atlantic Ocean, is also a Norwegian property. Within the Antarctic area, Norway claims Peter I Island and Queen Maud Land.

Norway spans approximately 1,089 miles (1,752 km) from its northernmost point to its southernmost point. Though Norway's coast is only 1,647 miles (2,650 km) long, it has many fjords and peninsulas. If the coast were straightened out, it would be 13,267 miles (21,351 km) long—approximately half the distance around the world.

The Arctic Circle divides the country almost in half. The area above this imaginary line is called the Land of the Midnight Sun because the sun shines continuously there during the height of summer.

Sweden, Finland, and Russia border Norway on the east. The Skagerrak—an arm of the North Sea—extends between Norway and Denmark in the south. Norway's western coast fronts on the North Sea in the south and the North Atlantic, or the Norwegian Sea, in the north. The Barents Sea, part of the Arctic Ocean, forms the country's northern frontier. The North Cape, which is located on Norway's Magerøya Island in the Arctic Ocean, is the northernmost point in Europe.

Topography

Norway can be divided into five main regions. In the north lie Trøndelag (the Trondheim region) and Nord Norge (North Norway).

Vestlandet (West Country) and Østlandet (East Country) fill the southern third of Norway. Sørlandet (South Country), at the southern tip of the nation, is the fifth region. Only about 20 percent of the country lies below an elevation of 500 feet (150 meters). The average altitude in Norway is about 1,500 feet (457 m) above sea level.

VESTLANDET, ØSTLANDET, AND SØRLANDET A north-south strip of mountains known as the Langfjella separates Østlandet from Vestlandet in southern Norway. Several ranges make up this mountainous chain. At the northern end is the Dovrefjell, and Jotunheimen rises in the central mountain region. Jotunheimen contains Galdhøpiggen (8,100 ft., 2,469 m), the highest peak in Scandinavia, and Glittertind (8,043 ft., 2,452 m), the second highest peak. West of

Romsdalhorn Mountain (4500 feet, 1550 m) *(above right)* is part of the Langfjella in Norway.

Jotunheimen is Jostedalsbreen, the largest glacier in Europe outside of Iceland. To the south is the Hardangervidda, a huge elevated plateau with an average height of about 3,300 feet (1,006 m).

In Vestlandet, the mountains descend steeply to the sea, and many fjords cut through the region. Geologists think that the fjords were formed when glaciers deepened the rivers in the area during the Ice Age (2 million to 10,000 years ago). Sogne Fjord, Norway's longest fjord at 127 miles (204 km) long, reaches depths of 4,000 feet (1,219 m) in some places, and its rock walls rise abruptly to more than 3,000 feet (914 m) above sea level.

Glittertind was once the highest mountain peak in Scandinavia, but it is losing elevation as its glacier melts away. At the beginning of the twenty-first century, Galdhøpiggen is officially 57 feet (19 m) taller.

Lowlands lie along the southern coast of Bokn Fjord in the southwest, along the lower part of Hardanger Fjord south of Bergen, and on coastal islands. These areas contain most of Vestlandet's population and farmland. A *strandflat*, or rock shelf, lies just below sea level offshore. This feature forms islands, some of which are inhabited, at points where the shelf rises just above sea level.

The gradual, eastern slopes of the Langfjella make up the valleys and rolling hills of Østlandet. Some of Norway's best agricultural land lies in the lower parts of these eastern valleys, particularly around the Oslo Fjord. Several valleys, such as Hallingdalen and Gudbrandsdalen, connect Østlandet and Vestlandet.

Sørlandet covers the extreme southern tip of Norway and includes the city of Kristiansand as well as many small communities. Summers in this region offer warm, sunny weather, and the rocky, island-studded south coast—with its many bays and coves—attracts Norwegian boaters and vacationers. The county of Telemark and its surrounding region is famed as the birthplace of skiing.

TRØNDELAG AND NORD NORGE Trøndelag, located north of the highest mountains, resembles Østlandet, with several wide valleys converging from the north. The broad Trondheim Fjord is the main landscape feature of this region. Many peninsulas and bays shelter the fjord from the sea, and rich farmland surrounds the waterway. This region has long been a major area of settlement.

Fjords and mountains characterize the vast expanse of Nord Norge. The Kjølen Mountains extend along the border with Sweden. In

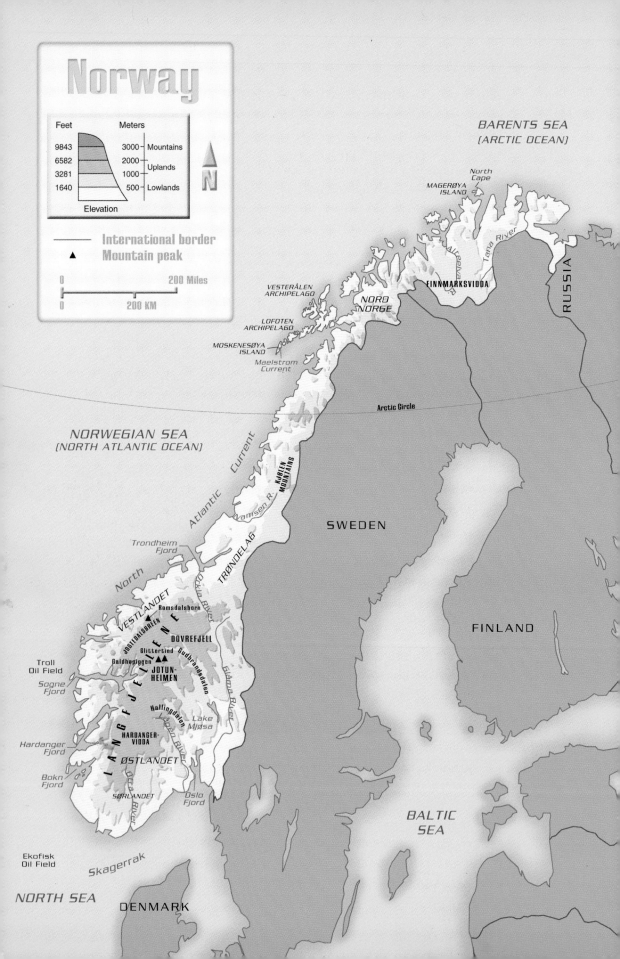

Norway

Feet	Meters	
9843	3000	Mountains
6582	2000	Uplands
3281	1000	
1640	500	Lowlands

Elevation

N

―――― International border
▲ Mountain peak

0 ——————— 200 Miles
0 ——————— 200 KM

BARENTS SEA
[ARCTIC OCEAN]

North
Cape

MAGERØYA
ISLAND

Altaelva

Tana River

FINNMARKSVIDDA

RUSSIA

VESTERÅLEN
ARCHIPELAGO

NORD
NORGE

LOFOTEN
ARCHIPELAGO

MOSKENESØYA
ISLAND

Maelstrom
Current

Arctic Circle

NORWEGIAN SEA
[NORTH ATLANTIC OCEAN]

Atlantic Current

KJØLEN MOUNTAINS

Namsen R.

SWEDEN

FINLAND

Trondheim
Fjord

North

TRØNDELAG

Orkla River

Troll
Oil Field

Sogne
Fjord

VESTLANDET

Romsdalshorn
JOSTEDALSBREEN ▲

LANGFJELLENE

DOVREFJELL

Glittertind ▲▲
Galdhøpiggen ▲
JOTUN-
HEIMEN

Gudbrandsdalen

Glåma River

Hallingdalen

Lågen River

Lake
Mjøsa

Hardanger
Fjord

HARDANGER-
VIDDA

ØSTLANDET

Lågen River

Bokn
Fjord

SØRLANDET

Oslo
Fjord

FINLAND

Ekofisk
Oil Field

Skagerrak

BALTIC
SEA

NORTH SEA

DENMARK

northernmost Nord Norge, which faces the Arctic Ocean, the land rises up from the fjords to the Finnmarksvidda—an area of bleak mountain plateaus and glaciers.

A sparsely populated region, Nord Norge has towns primarily along the coast and on nearby islands, which are part of the strandflat. The Lofoten and Vesterålen Archipelagoes, Norway's largest coastal island groups, are actually the peaks of an ancient volcanic mountain range that lies mostly underwater. The Mælstrom Current (Moskstraumen in Norwegian) that passes between the two outermost Lofoten islands can form dangerous whirlpools.

Rivers and Lakes

Numerous rivers in Norway have cut valleys through the mountains. Waterways that descend to the southwest from the steep western slopes are generally short, with many rapids and waterfalls. In Østlandet, the rivers tend to be longer and travel southeastward at a gentler angle.

The longest river in Norway is the 380-mile (611-km) Glåma, which begins in the Dovrefjell and flows south into the Skagerrak at the city of Fredrikstad. Other waterways include the Alteelva and Tana Rivers in the north, the Orkla and Namsen in Trøndelag, and the Lågen and Otra in the south. For centuries, the largest rivers

Norway's rugged landscape features many **waterfalls and rapids.**

in southeastern Norway, such as the Glåma, have been used to float timber and to produce power for sawmills and grain mills. Although few of the waterways are navigable, they are a valuable source of hydroelectric power.

Many small lakes that were formed by glaciers dot the Norwegian countryside. The largest of these bodies of water is Lake Mjøsa, which covers 142 square miles (368 sq. km) in southeastern Norway.

Climate

Norway's climate is surprisingly mild for its location astride the Arctic Circle. The moderate weather is due to the North Atlantic Current, a branch of the Gulf Stream Current, which travels along the Norwegian coast. Originating in the Caribbean Sea, the waters of the Gulf Stream are warmed by the hot Caribbean sun, which makes them about 15 Fahrenheit degrees (8 Celsius degrees) warmer than the surrounding ocean. In winter, the Gulf Stream warms the cold westerly winds that blow toward Europe. These gusts, in turn, make coastal regions of Norway as much as 45°F (7°C) warmer in January than the world average for the same latitude.

As a result of this warm-water current, winter temperatures in the coastal regions usually exceed 25°F (−4°C), except in the extreme north, where they may drop down to 18°F (−8°C). Snow that falls along the coast melts almost immediately, and most of Norway's seaports are free of ice all year. In the summertime, however, the ocean cools the air along the western coast, and the temperature generally stays in the mid-fifties (12° to 14°C).

Inland, the differences between summer and winter become greater because the mountains shield these regions from the moderating influence of the ocean. Readings for the innermost regions range from 10° to 18°F (−12° to −8°C) in January. In the far north, inland temperatures fall below 10°F (−12°C). Snow covers the ground for at least three months of the year in colder regions. Summers are warmest around the capital city of Oslo and along the southeastern coast, which has average temperatures in the sixties (16° to 21°C) in July. The mountains and the extreme north have the coolest summer weather, with temperatures generally below 54°F (12°C).

A few areas in Norway—mainly in the upper reaches of the eastern valleys—are so dry that farmers must irrigate to raise crops. Most of the country, however, receives plenty of moisture throughout the year. Coastal regions get about 70 inches (178 centimeters) of precipitation annually, while less than 40 inches (102 cm) fall in areas east of the mountains. The Bergen region on the western coast records the heaviest amounts of rainfall.

At noon in midwinter, a **Finnmark dogsled team** makes good use of the brief twilight near Karasjok. To learn more about the Arctic Circle, go to vgsbooks.com for links.

Because Norway lies so far north, the seasonal change in the number of daylight hours is much greater than it is in lands near the equator. As the earth revolves around the Sun, regions close to the North and South Poles alternate between facing completely into or entirely away from the Sun's light. The area north of the Arctic Circle is known as the Land of the Midnight Sun because daylight lasts continuously from mid-May through July. From mid-November through January, on the other hand, the region experiences continuous darkness.

Flora and Fauna

Because of its diverse landscapes, contrasting climates, and varying altitudes, Norway hosts a wide range of plants—about two thousand species. A few mountain plants grow only in Norway, but most species are common to other countries as well. In the far north and at high elevations are tundra regions, where the topsoil thaws only for a short period every year. Common plants here are dwarf birch, mosses, and lichens. The richest vegetation in Norway is found in the southeast along Oslo Fjord and near large lakes such as Mjøsa. Mushrooms and wild berries—including blueberries, lingonberries, and cranberries— grow in wooded areas. Rare outside Scandinavia is the cloudberry (a relative of the blackberry), which hikers gather in mountain areas.

Norwegian forests, which cover more than one-fifth of the land area, abound in fir and pine. Deciduous (leaf-shedding) forests consisting of oak, ash, hazel, elm, and linden are located in the south and southwest. In some places, birch, yew, and evergreen holly thrive. The coasts and the eastern and central valleys are thick with Scotch pine and Norway spruce. Birch, alder, aspen, and mountain ash also grow in these regions.

Animal life in the tundra includes reindeer, polar foxes, polar hares, wolves, wolverines, and lemmings. Every eleven or twelve years, the lemming population increases suddenly and dramatically, so that thousands of the rodents fall to their death by swarming off cliff edges. Elk, deer, foxes, otters, and marten inhabit the south and southeast.

About three hundred species of birds nest in Norway for at least part of the year. Some of these—certain kinds of hawks, falcons, and eagles, for example—are endangered species. The law protects white-tailed and golden eagles. Millions of seabirds—including puffins, gulls, gannets, and fulmars—breed on cliffs that overlook the ocean.

Some wild herds of **reindeer** remain in Norway and neighboring Scandinavian countries, but most reindeer are descendants of herds domesticated up to seven thousand years ago.

Atlantic puffins spend most of their lives at sea in the North Atlantic Ocean. However, many individuals come ashore in Norway to breed. Females lay just one egg per season.

Both freshwater and saltwater fish abound in Norway. Salmon, trout, grayling, perch, and pike swim in the rivers and lakes. Herring, cod, and mackerel are among the species that inhabit the coastal waters.

Cities and Towns

Although Oslo is Norway's only major urban center, smaller cities dot the countryside. Stavanger, Kristiansand, Drammen, Skien, Tromsø, and Bodø have populations of between 30,000 and 110,000. Honningsvåg (population 2,900) was recently designated as a town and replaced Hammerfest (population 10,000) as the northernmost town in the world.

OSLO The capital city of Oslo sits at the inner tip of Oslo Fjord, which stretches 60 miles (96 km) inland from the southern coast. King Harald III founded Oslo in about A.D. 1050. After a fire destroyed the city in 1624, King Christian IV rebuilt it, and residents renamed it Christiania in honor of their ruler. The original name, Oslo, was restored in 1925.

Oslo has served as Norway's capital since the nation achieved complete independence from Sweden in 1905. It is also the country's principal commercial, industrial, and cultural center. With a population of about 507,500, the city covers 175 square miles (453 sq. km). Forests and lakes take up more than two-thirds of this area, which makes Oslo an ideal recreation center. Major industries in the capital include shipbuilding and the production of chemicals, machinery, metal, and paper.

Karl Johans gate, Oslo's main street, descends from the Royal Palace *(left)* past the Grand Hotel *(clock tower, right)* to the central railway station.

Karl Johans gate, the main street that runs through the middle of the city, passes the stately Grand Hotel, the yellow-brick Parliament Building, the University of Oslo, and the National Theater. The thoroughfare stretches from the central railway station to the gardens of the Royal Palace. Several museums and galleries—the National Gallery, Frogner Park (a sculpture park), the open-air Folk Museum, and the Viking Ship Museum, for example—attract both Norwegians and foreigners.

Norwegians love the outdoors, and Oslo residents have it especially good. They are reluctant to leave the city—which lies in the middle of the Nordmarka forest area—because they love taking walks through the woods. This condition is known as the **Nordmarka syndrome.**

SECONDARY CITIES Set in a valley at the foot of seven mountains, Bergen is Norway's second largest city, with a population of about 229,500. Founded in A.D. 1070 by King Olaf (or Olav) III, Bergen has many historic buildings that date back to the twelfth century. The city remains rich in tradition, despite several fires throughout its history and severe damage during World War II (1939–1945). The chief seaport of western Norway,

Fresh fish is for sale six days a week at an open-air market *(far right)* at Vagen, **Bergen's main harbor.**

Bergen is a cultural, fishing, industrial, and shipping center. Factories in the city manufacture steel, ships, fishing equipment, processed food, forest products, and electrical machinery.

The oldest city in Norway, Trondheim has more than 149,000 residents, making it the third largest urban area in the country. Founded in A.D. 997 by King Olaf I, Trondheim (then known as Nidaros) served as Norway's capital until 1380. The city's most important landmark is the Nidaros Cathedral, an eleventh-century cathedral built over the tomb of King Olaf II, Norway's patron saint. A commercial hub for the surrounding agricultural area, Trondheim is also an export center for copper, iron ore, timber, and fish.

The **Nidaros Cathedral** in Trondheim burned twice in the eighteenth century. Full restoration from its surviving medieval fragments began in 1869, and the final statue was installed in 1983.

HISTORY AND GOVERNMENT

Scientists have found evidence of the beginnings of human life in Norway that dates to the end of the last Ice Age, as many as twelve thousand years ago. As the ice of the Ice Age melted away and land was exposed, people traveled up and down the coast looking for the best place to survive—where food and shelter were the easiest to come by. The first written records of Norwegian history date from about A.D. 800.

The oldest finds come from Finnmark, the northernmost county in Norway, and from Møre og Romsdal county in northwestern Vestlandet. The inhabitants of these areas probably hunted and fished for food, and they fashioned tools from bone, antlers, and stone. Although their origins are unknown, these peoples may have reached Norway from across the narrow Kola Peninsula in northern Russia. Another route might have brought the newcomers from central Europe by way of Denmark and Sweden, which at that time were connected to each other by land.

The Rise of Permanent Settlements

Until about 3000 B.C., the peoples of Norway lived in tents or in mountain caves along the coast. They lived by hunting and fishing. Between 3000 and 1500 B.C., warlike Germanic groups migrated to Norway. From them the local inhabitants learned to attach handles to their axes, which made the tools more efficient in work and in battle. During this period, the people also began to keep cattle and to grow grain. As farming became a way of life, the inhabitants of Norway no longer needed to roam in search of food.

Permanent farming settlements arose along the coast and around lakes. Fjords and mountains isolated these communities from one another. As a result, they became independent realms, each with its own leader. Eventually, aristocracies (small, ruling classes) developed, and kings emerged from these privileged groups to head the communities. By the A.D. 700s, about thirty small kingdoms existed in Norway.

The Viking Age

After A.D. 600, Norway entered a period of rapid population growth, perhaps because Germanic peoples had moved to Scandinavia in the previous two centuries. The population increase led to shortages of farmland, and the inhabitants began to take an interest in other regions. By about 800 (and possibly much sooner), Norwegians, Danes, and Swedes began to travel abroad, conquering territory and expanding their trade markets. The Scandinavians of this period, which lasted until about 1050, later became known as Vikings. The term may have come from *vik*, the Norse word for "fjord" or "bay." It could also be a form of the Old English word *wic*, which means "soldier" or "trader."

Warlike raids, which small groups carried out against various other European communities, marked the first hundred years of the Viking Age. These acts gave the Vikings a reputation of being pirates. Gradually, however, their expeditions abroad became larger and more organized, with armies and navies under the command of chieftains.

Vikings traveled great distances in all directions. Russia's name is derived from what local inhabitants called the Viking leader Rurik while he controlled eastern Russia. Visit vgsbooks.com for links to additional information on the Vikings and their ships.

Despite their reputation for being aggressive, not all Vikings were warriors. The majority worked most of the time as farmers or in occupations such as shipbuilding, metalworking, or fishing. Viking traders sailed to many parts of the world in swift, lightweight wooden vessels that ranked among the best boats of their time. In fact, trade eventually became the primary activity of the Vikings.

Viking Expeditions

One of the first recorded Viking attacks occurred in 793, when Norwegians plundered a monastery on the island of Lindisfarne, off the eastern coast of England. After that, Norwegians began raiding England, Ireland, the Isle of Man, and Scotland. Ireland, with its fertile land and rich churches, was a choice target for attack. During the mid-800s, Norwegian raiders also looted and burned towns in France, Italy, and Spain.

By the late 800s, Viking expeditions had become more peaceful. Paths traveled by earlier pirates became active trade routes. Some Norwegians turned to the North Atlantic, exploring and emigrating to uninhabited islands—the Færoes and Iceland. From Iceland, a Norwegian explorer named Erik Thorvaldson (Erik the Red) sailed to Greenland in 982, and a few years later he established two settlements there. Eventually, Norway added the Færoes, Iceland, and Greenland to its kingdom.

In about 1000, Leif Eriksson, son of Erik the Red, led an expedition farther west and landed on the eastern coast of North America. Eriksson called the territory Vinland and established a settlement in what later became the Canadian island of Newfoundland. However, this first European colony on the North American continent (in

VIKING BURIAL

In 1904 a Viking longship was excavated in Vestfold county. The ship was made of oak and was 72 feet (22 m) long and had a crew of thirty-five. The remains of a Viking woman, who had received a noble burial, were found in the ship. She was buried with kitchen utensils, weaving equipment, chests, caskets, tapestries, furniture, clothing, and other items, many of which were richly decorated. She was also buried with the bodies of a female slave (who was sacrificed for the burial) and several horses and dogs. Studies indicate that the ship was buried in the 830s. Archaeologists and historians argue about who the woman was. Some experts believe she was Queen Åsa, the grandmother of Harald Fairhair, the first king of Norway.

The **first Vikings to land on the North American continent** are believed to have been part of a comparatively peaceful migration of livestock farmers across the North Atlantic.

modern times known as L'Anse aux Meadows), was soon abandoned because of attacks on the newcomers from local inhabitants. Nevertheless, Greenlanders continued expeditions to Vinland to gather timber until the mid-fourteenth century. After the fifteenth century, the Norwegian population on Greenland died out, and Norway lost contact with North America.

Attempts to Unify Norway

Shortly before 900, King Harald Fairhair (Harald I), from a realm in southeastern Norway, defeated many regional chieftains and kings. The unity he achieved, however, was short lived. After his death in 933, his sons shared control of the kingdom, with Erik Bloodaxe as the supreme ruler. Conflict erupted among the heirs, and many of the regional leaders refused to surrender their independence. While these domestic struggles were occurring, both Denmark and Sweden sought Norwegian territory.

Olaf Tryggvason (Olaf I), a great-grandson of Harald I, ascended the throne in 995. As a youth, Olaf I had lived in England, where he adopted the Roman Catholic religion. After he became king, Olaf I tried to impose his Christian faith on his subjects, killing those who would not accept it. In 1000, at the naval battle of Svold, the forces of Denmark and

Sweden united with dissatisfied Norwegian leaders to defeat and kill Olaf I. The victors divided his land among themselves.

In 1015 Olaf Haraldsson (Olaf II) drove out the foreigners, reunited Norway, and made himself king. Olaf II continued to force Christianity upon Norwegians, and pagans (those who, like the Vikings, worshiped many gods) who resisted were executed. Pagan places of worship were destroyed. As he increased his power, Olaf II created many enemies among the nobles. This group united with Canute II, king of Denmark and England, and in 1030 killed Olaf II at the Battle of Stiklestad, northeast of Trondheim. Olaf's death put Norway in Danish hands.

The Roman Catholic Church canonized **Olaf II** (declared him a saint) in 1164 for his efforts to Christianize Norway.

Danish rulers imposed heavy taxes, and Norwegians grew discontented with foreign control. They began to think of Olaf II as a hero for his efforts to unite the country, despite his cruel enforcement of Christianity. Much later, Catholic authorities in Rome elevated Olaf II to sainthood. By proclaiming him a saint, the Church aroused even greater national pride among Norwegians, and Christianity became firmly rooted in the country.

Three Centuries of Self-Rule

After King Canute died in 1035, Norwegians hailed Olaf II's son Magnus as Norway's king. Magnus I united Norway and Denmark under his rule. For the next three centuries, Norwegian kings ruled Norway. During this period, the Roman Catholic Church grew in power, foreign trade expanded, and Norwegian religious and trading centers developed into important cities. Political chaos and bitter struggles for royal power also came about, partly because all the sons of a king had equal rights to succession.

From 1130 to 1240, civil wars ravaged the country as nobles from different regions unsuccessfully tried to gain the throne. In 1184 Sverre Sigurdsson became king and reestablished the role of the monarch as the supreme ruler of the land. This move weakened the power of the Church. Religious leaders opposed Sverre's reign, and another round of civil wars began. Haakon Haakonsson (Haakon IV), Sverre's successor, restored lasting peace in 1240, when he killed his main rival at a battle near Trondheim.

In 1250 Haakon IV granted trading privileges to a group of northern German merchant cities known as the Hanseatic League. Gradually, this organization took control of Norwegian trade, and the country depended on the league for imports of grain. The monarchs of this period increased their power and restricted succession to the throne to the oldest legitimate son of a king.

When Haakon Magnusson (Haakon V) became king in 1299, he established his royal residence in Oslo. Haakon V built several castles to help fortify the country. To ensure his own power, Haakon V eliminated the titles of earl and baron from the aristocracy and ruled without the advice of nobles. As a result, the nobility gradually declined.

Haakon V had no male heirs. When he died in 1319, the throne went to the son of his daughter, who had married a Swedish prince. Magnus Eriksson (Magnus VII) thus became king of both Norway and Sweden. Magnus VII lived in Sweden, however, and neglected Norwegian affairs. During his reign, in 1349 and 1350, the bubonic plague swept across Norway, killing at least half the population.

The remaining fifty-eight **Hanseatic League buildings in Bergen,** collectively known as Bryggen, became a World Heritage Site in 1979.

Survivors of the epidemic faced famine and severe economic problems. To satisfy Norwegian demands for more consideration of their needs, Magnus VII gave the Norwegian throne to his son Haakon in 1355. Haakon VI was the last king of an independent Norway until 1905.

○ Union with Denmark

After Haakon VI died in 1380, his wife, Margaret, who was the ruler of Denmark, became the queen of Norway as well. In 1388, amid political instability in Sweden, Swedish nobles elected her to rule their country. In 1397 Margaret formally united Norway, Denmark, and Sweden in the Union of Kalmar. Sweden revolted against Danish rule several times and eventually broke away from the union in 1523. Norway, however, remained under Danish control for the next four centuries.

During the union with Denmark, Norway grew weaker politically as Denmark increased its strength. The Norwegian national council, a body of advisors to the Danish government, began to lose influence. In 1536 Denmark declared Norway a Danish province and dissolved the national council altogether, thereby stripping the country of its voice in Norwegian affairs. Denmark's leaders also made Lutheranism—a newly formed sect that had broken away from the Roman Catholic Church—the official religion of Norway.

Despite Danish control, Norway's economy began to prosper in the sixteenth century as Norwegians discovered a European market for their vast reserves of timber. As a result, the Norwegian shipping industry expanded rapidly during the sixteenth and seventeenth centuries. A class of wealthy townspeople arose, and the number of port cities increased.

Norway prospered in peace throughout the eighteenth century, until the territorial goals of the French general Napoleon Bonaparte pitted nations against one another. When Napoleon set out to conquer Europe during the Napoleonic Wars (1804–1814), Denmark sided with France against Great Britain. Britain, which had been Norway's chief trading partner, used its naval forces to prevent ships from landing in Norway. Norwegian trade stopped, and many Norwegians starved. Because the blockade cut off Norway from Denmark, Norwegians began to manage their own affairs, and they secretly resumed trade with the British.

Sweden, an ally of Britain, defeated Denmark in 1813. According to the Treaty of Kiel, Denmark gave Norway to Sweden but kept Norway's island colonies—Iceland, Greenland, and the Færoes. At first Norway refused to recognize the treaty. Instead, it declared independence and adopted a Norwegian constitution on May 17, 1814. Sweden, however, would not accept Norwegian independence and attacked and quickly defeated Norwegian troops. In November 1814, the Norwegian Storting (parliament) accepted King Charles XIII of Sweden as Norway's ruler. Charles promised to uphold the Norwegian constitution.

In 1814 the Norwegian government agreed to accept Swedish king Charles XIII as their ruler.

◉ Union with Sweden

Although Sweden controlled Norway's foreign affairs, it granted Norway a great deal of internal independence. A Norwegian cabinet advised the Swedish king on matters that affected Norway, and local governing councils were set up in Norwegian communities.

During the nineteenth century, Norway began to develop textile, paper, and fish-canning industries. At the same time, the nation constructed railways and roads, which made it easier to transport these products throughout the country. Expansion of the merchant marine, which shipped goods around the globe, made Norway active in world trade. By 1870 Norway's merchant marine had become the third largest in the world. These economic developments transformed Norwegian agriculture into a business in which farmers produced crops for sale rather than to feed only their families.

Despite these improvements, Norway's economic growth could not keep pace with a population that more than doubled during the nineteenth century. Between 1866 and 1915, more than 600,000 Norwegians emigrated to North America in search of jobs and cheap, fertile land. No other country except Ireland saw such a high percentage of its population leave for the United States. The 1880s were especially hard years, and many people could not find jobs.

Norwegian emigration to the United States began in earnest when the U.S. Congress passed the Homestead Act in 1862. The act granted new settlers up to 160 acres (65 hectares) of land to farm. Norwegians in America wrote letters to friends and relatives in Norway praising their new country. Their letters often encouraged entire Norwegian towns to join them in America.

The rapid departure of so many Norwegians forced the government to examine its policies. The Storting enacted social legislation in the late nineteenth and early twentieth centuries, partly to satisfy Norwegians who were tempted to emigrate. Democratic reforms such as unemployment relief, improvement in factory conditions, expansion of public schools, and the emergence of strong trade unions improved living conditions for average citizens.

In 1884 the liberal Venstre (Left) and conservative Høyre (Right) political parties were formed. A few years later, the Norwegian Labor Party entered the political arena. Johan Sverdrup, founder of the Venstre Party and president of the Storting, united rural Norwegians and encouraged them to speak up for their needs. The right to vote was extended to all men over the age of twenty-five in 1898, and women gained equal voting rights in 1913.

Along with the nineteenth-century liberal democratic movement arose nationalistic sentiments. Norwegians grew increasingly discontented with their inferior political position in the union with Sweden. They sought greater freedom, particularly in foreign affairs. Literature and intellectual activity began to reflect a distinct Norwegian identity. Bjørnstjerne Bjørnson, who wrote the Norwegian national anthem, Henrik Wergeland, and Henrik Ibsen were among the spokespeople for this cultural rebirth.

Independence

As Norwegians strengthened their national identity and political power, they grew bolder in their demands on Sweden. In 1892 the Venstre majority in the Storting passed a resolution to establish an independent consular service. This meant Norway could send its own representatives to foreign countries to protect Norwegian business interests. The Swedish king Oscar II vetoed the resolution, and negotiations about the terms of the Swedish-Norwegian union led nowhere. In response, Norwegian leaders decided to strengthen their position by building up their military.

King Oscar II still refused to grant consular service to Norway, and in 1905 the Norwegian cabinet resigned. Because the Norwegian constitution allowed the king to exercise royal power only through a cabinet, the resignation of the cabinet left King Oscar II powerless in Norway. In effect, Norway no longer had a king, and the union between Sweden and Norway therefore no longer existed.

At first the Swedish government refused to dissolve the union, but it agreed to reconsider the matter if a general election in Norway proved that a majority of the Norwegian people desired independence. Norwegians voted almost unanimously for self-rule, and Sweden agreed to recognize Norwegian independence in September 1905.

After debating whether to establish a monarchy or a republic, a majority of Norwegians voted to install a king. Since the Norwegians had no royalty of their own, they elected Prince Charles of Denmark (who was not in line to inherit the Danish throne) as their king. He took the name Haakon VII, thereby continuing a line of kings that had ended with the formation of the union with Denmark upon the death of Haakon VI in 1380.

1900 to 1945

During the early years of independence, Norway underwent a rapid transition from an economy founded on agriculture to one based on

Norway's royal family, Haakon VII *(standing),* his wife Princess Maud, and their son Olav (the future king Olav V) posed for this photograph in the early 1900s.

manufacturing and trade. Industries that processed metals and chemicals developed in addition to the existing textile and food-processing plants. Hydroelectric power stations were built along the nation's many rivers to fuel the emerging factories.

The newly independent nation also made great strides in social legislation, education, and political liberties, setting an example that many European countries would later follow. Norway became famous for welfare policies such as unemployment benefits, retirement pensions, and liberal laws concerning divorce and illegitimacy (children born out of wedlock).

During World War I (1914–1918), Norway, Sweden, and Denmark agreed to remain neutral and to cooperate for their mutual interest. The friendship established during this period continued after the war.

When the war ended, Norway experienced an economic decline, and the worldwide depression that began in 1929 worsened the nation's financial situation. One-fourth to one-third of the nation's workers were unemployed during the 1930s.

German infantry follow a tank through the snow during the assault on Norway in 1940.

When World War II began in 1939, Norway maintained its traditional policy of neutrality. The Germans forced Norway into the war, however, when they invaded the country on April 9, 1940. Assisted by Vidkun Quisling and other disloyal Norwegian army officers, the Germans attacked all of Norway's important ports. After two months of fighting, Norway surrendered, and King Haakon VII and his cabinet fled to London, where they formed a government in exile. Germany installed Josef Terboven as its commissioner in Norway.

The Norwegian people strongly resisted the repressive measures of the German occupation. They also aided the efforts of the Allied powers against Germany.

The Nazis demanded complete acceptance of German occupation, but the Norwegian people resisted. Almost all of the bishops in the Church of Norway resigned from their official positions but continued their parish work in secret. Though the press was censored, people produced secret newspapers. Eleven hundred teachers were arrested because they refused to cooperate with the Nazis.

On May 8, 1945, after Germany was defeated elsewhere, the German forces in Norway surrendered. King Haakon returned to Norway on June 7, the fortieth anniversary of Norwegian independence. In order to punish traitors, the government restored the death penalty, which had been abolished in 1876. Quisling, whose name had become an international word for traitor, was tried in court and executed for treason along with about twenty-five other Norwegians. About ten thousand Norwegians had died during the war, about half the merchant fleet had sunk, and the northern counties of Troms and Finnmark lay largely in ruins.

▶ Postwar Developments

After the war, Norway became a charter member of the United Nations (UN), an organization of nations that works for world peace and security. The Norwegian Trygve Lie became the UN's first secretary-general. In 1949 Norway also joined the North Atlantic Treaty Organization (NATO), a regional defense alliance.

Aided by loans from the United States, Norway rebuilt its industries and its merchant fleet. The government, led by the Labor Party, carefully planned the entire economy. The nation strengthened its position in international markets and redistributed wealth more equally among its citizens. By the 1950s, the Norwegian economy was thriving as it shifted from an emphasis on industries to a focus on services such as health care and banking.

In the mid-1950s, the Nordic countries (Denmark, Finland, Iceland, Norway, and Sweden) formed the Nordic Council. This organization has fostered much cooperation among the member countries, primarily on economic, social, and cultural issues. To further secure their well-being, Norway and six other countries formed an economic union called the European Free Trade Association (EFTA) in 1959.

New social legislation accompanied economic growth and greatly improved the welfare of Norwegians. In 1966 the Storting passed the National Insurance Act—one of the most important reforms in Norwegian history. A social security plan, this program covers

United Nations secretary-general **Trygve Lie** from Norway *(near right)* and General Anastasio Somoza from Nicaragua *(far right)* confer at the United Nations in New York City in 1952.

retirement pensions and job retraining. The act also gives aid to mothers, orphans, widows, widowers, and handicapped persons.

In 1969 an exploration team discovered oil off Norway's North Sea coast. In the next decade, the state began to extract petroleum and natural gas, and since then the economy has depended on the export of these products. While fossil fuel production is predicted to rise, the reliance on these products for the nation's income threatens economic stability because the supply is limited and because oil prices are often unpredictable.

International Role

Throughout the 1980s, the Norwegian government adopted strict antipollution laws, and Prime Minister Gro Harlem Brundtland became an international leader of the debate on environmental issues. Yet severe pollution continues to affect Norwegian lakes, forests, and wildlife. Pollution from foreign sources, such as factory smoke from Great Britain, has caused strained relations between Norway and its neighbors. In addition, Norwegian leaders disagree on the economic costs and benefits of stricter environmental laws.

As the twentieth century closed, Norway took a more prominent role in international politics. It forged the Oslo Agreement between Israel and the Palestine Liberation Organization and fostered talks between the Sri Lankan government and Tamil Tiger rebels, who were fighting for a separate Tamil state. However, in some ways Norway remains an isolated nation. In 1994 Norwegians voted against joining the European Union (EU), an economic partnership of European countries, even though their government strongly urged them to vote "yes." It was the second time Norway had voted on and rejected membership to the EU. The first vote was in 1972.

Since Norway began exporting oil, it has been one of the richest countries in the world, but citizens

POLLUTION

Norway's problems with pollution started in the 1960s, when rapid economic expansion resulted in increased sewage production, emissions from industry, and agricultural waste runoff. The increased emissions threatened life in lakes, rivers, and fjords. Acid rain from Great Britain and the rest of Europe has ruined thousands of fishing lakes in southern Norway.

Worse yet, in 2001 radioactive waste from a nuclear reactor was found in a town's sewage system. The waste dumping had been going on for nine years before it was detected.

Norwegians **Kjell Magne Bondevik** and **Dr. Gro Harlem Brundtland** are active international leaders. Elected prime minister of Norway in 2001, Bondevik faces domestic as well as international challenges. In 1998 former prime minister Brundtland became the director-general of the World Health Organization.

have grown angry over high tax rates, deteriorating public services, and the high cost of living. As a result, voters forced a change of government four times between 1996 and 2001. In 2001 the Labor Party, traditionally the strongest in the country (and in power for most of the twentieth century), took a particularly sharp hit from voters, leaving it in control of only 24 percent of the Storting, down from 35 percent in the previous election.

Government

Norway is a constitutional and hereditary monarchy, under King Harald V and Queen Sonja. Both men and women can inherit the throne. The monarch is the head of state, but the monarch's role is mainly ceremonial. The monarch is the supreme commander of the Norwegian armed forces and also is the head of the Church of Norway—which is Evangelical Lutheran and to which the monarch and at least half of the executive cabinet must belong.

In 1901 the Nobel Prize was established as "an award to those who in the past year had done the most good for mankind." Most Nobel prizes (such as the physics award) are awarded by Swedish institutions. The responsibility for awarding the **Nobel Peace Prize**, however, belongs to an independent committee appointed by the Norwegian Storting.

In terms of real power, however, Norway operates as a parliamentary democracy. Executive power is exercised through a prime minister and a cabinet. The ruling monarch appoints the prime minister, who is usually the leader of the political party holding the most seats in the Storting. The prime minister, in turn, appoints seventeen cabinet ministers, who head the various governmental departments. Cabinet members sit in the Storting, but they do not vote. After the shakeup election of 2001, Kjell Magne Bondevik, of the Christian People's Party, emerged as the new prime minister. Bondevik is a Lutheran pastor and has served as prime minister before. He had resigned from the position in 2000.

All Norwegian citizens who are eighteen or older can participate in parliamentary elections, which are held every four years. Each of Norway's nineteen counties elects four to fifteen Storting members, depending on the size of the local population. Oslo, which is considered a county, elects fifteen members. Finnmark, the least populous county, elects four.

The Storting consists of one house, but its 165 members form two sections—the Lagting and the Odelsting—to discuss and vote on proposed legislation. If the two sections do not agree on a piece of legislation, it can be approved by a two-thirds majority of the entire parliament. Some matters can be decided only by the entire Storting.

The highest judicial body in Norway is the supreme court, which consists of a president and seventeen judges. Below this, five regional courts of appeal hear the most serious cases as well as appeals of decisions made by county and town courts. Conciliation councils handle civil suits, and county and town courts determine criminal cases. The monarch appoints judges to all of the courts except the conciliation courts, whose members are elected locally.

A government official called an ombudsman investigates complaints made by citizens about governmental actions or decisions. The office was established to provide an impartial and informal method of handling unfair treatment against individuals.

For administrative purposes, Norway is divided into nineteen *fylker*, or counties—one of which is the city of Oslo. Each *fylke* except Oslo has a governor named by the monarch. The fylker, in turn, are divided into rural and urban *kommuner*, or districts. Community councils, which are elected every fourth year, run the local districts. County councils consist of members of the community councils.

The **Storting building,** where the Storting (parliament) meets, was completed in 1866, following thirty years of disagreement over its design and location. It was designed by Swedish architect Emil Victor Langlet.

THE PEOPLE

Most of Norway's 4.5 million inhabitants are closely related to the Danes, the Icelanders, and the Swedes. These peoples are descended from ancient groups that migrated to the region. Their ancestors came from lands east of the Baltic Sea, from around the Mediterranean Sea, or from the European Alps. Throughout the centuries, Norwegians intermarried with other groups, taking on various physical traits from these different peoples. Contrary to the popular image of fair-haired Norwegians, many of the nation's people have dark hair and brown eyes.

The Sami, an ethnic minority thought to be the first inhabitants of Norway, reside primarily in Nord Norge, but in modern times many live elsewhere. They arrived from central Asia thousands of years ago and have darker skin and a shorter stature than most Norwegians. Population estimates vary, but most officials agree that there are probably 70,000 Sami total, 40,000 of whom live in Norway. Their language, Sami, is related to Finnish.

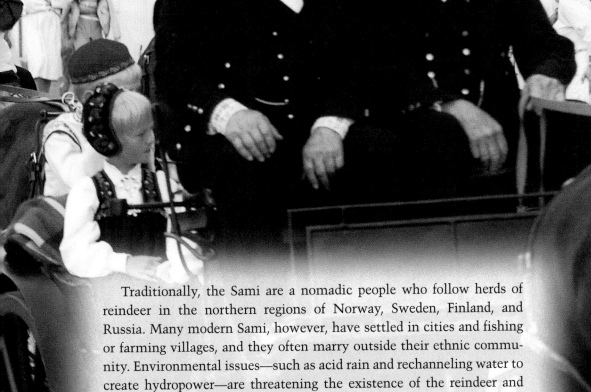

Traditionally, the Sami are a nomadic people who follow herds of reindeer in the northern regions of Norway, Sweden, Finland, and Russia. Many modern Sami, however, have settled in cities and fishing or farming villages, and they often marry outside their ethnic community. Environmental issues—such as acid rain and rechanneling water to create hydropower—are threatening the existence of the reindeer and therefore the lifestyle of the Sami.

Immigrants from southern Europe and various developing countries make up another minority in Norway. The nation depends on these immigrants to help fill its workforce. Many foreign workers and their families have taken up permanent residence in Norway, where they can enjoy a greatly improved standard of living. The government gives equal status to citizens and noncitizens living in Norway, so immigrants have equal access to such things as schooling and medical care.

In the past, most immigrants were from other European countries, especially from Scandinavian countries. In 1976 only 16 percent were from Asia, Africa, or South America. By 1990 that figure had risen to 41 percent. The increased immigration from developing countries has raised concerns in Norway. These immigrants tend to be poorer, less educated, and less skilled than earlier immigrants, and, therefore, they present a greater drain on social services. Some Norwegians believe that these new residents should be last in receiving jobs, housing, and other aid. The majority of Norwegians, however, are embarrassed by such intolerance.

Although the number and nationality of immigrants continue to increase, immigrants still make up less than 5 percent of the population. Even with these newcomers, the country has a population density of only 36 persons per square mile (14 per sq. km). About 74 percent of the nation's people live in cities.

◎ Social Welfare

The government of Norway provides its citizens with many welfare services. In fact, the nation has been a world leader in the establishment of state-funded health care, housing, employment benefits, retirement plans, and other services. Based on ideals of equality and justice, Norwegian legislation guarantees the rights to employment, a place to live, education, social security, and health and hospital services. Discrimination because of race, religion, gender, or political beliefs is prohibited. The government funds the welfare system through taxes and insurance, taking from those who earn the most and giving to those who need assistance. The result is a society in which few people are very rich or very poor.

All Norwegian families with children under the age of sixteen receive a yearly allowance for each child after their first. Financial aid is also available to help these families pay for housing. Large families with

Substantial tax breaks help families, such as these in Stavanger, lead satisfying lives.

medium or low incomes pay little or no state taxes, and their local taxes are reduced. The government guarantees all workers an annual four-week vacation with full pay.

All Norwegians are required to participate in the national insurance program, which covers many welfare options. The plan includes retirement funds, job retraining, and financial aid. An insurance program provides free medical care and pays cash to employees when illness prevents them from working. Insured workers, their employers, and both national and local governments share the cost of all state insurance plans.

Health Care

Because it ensures a minimum standard of living for all its citizens, Norway has no severe health problems. Once plagued by polio and tuberculosis, modern Norwegians mainly face the risk of illnesses such as cancer and heart disease, which are common to wealthy industrialized countries. To combat tuberculosis and other contagious illnesses, all children receive complete vaccinations, and the entire population is given periodic tuberculin tests from infancy onward. About 0.1 percent of Norwegians between the ages of 15 and 49 suffer from HIV (human immunodeficiency virus) or AIDS (acquired immunodeficiency syndrome).

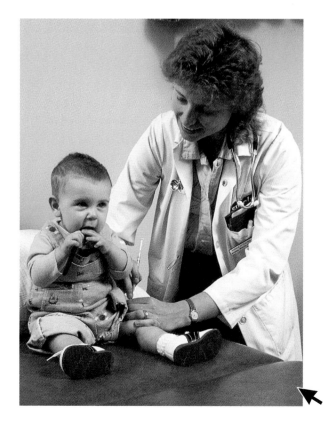

In the early 2000s, a Norwegian's life expectancy at birth was estimated to be 78 years. One factor is Norway's **child vaccination** program.

Measures of health improved markedly in the twentieth century. In the 1890s, the average life expectancy for Norwegians was only 52 years, but by 2001 that figure had risen to 78 years. At the end of the nineteenth century, roughly 100 infants died out of every 1,000 born. By 2001 an average of 3.9 babies died out of each 1,000 live births, which is among the best ratios in the world.

Like many industrialized nations, Norway experienced a low birthrate—13 births per 1,000 people—in 2001. Fewer Norwegian women are choosing to have large families, if they have children at all. As a result, Norway's annual growth rate is just over 0.5 percent.

With a national insurance plan that covers virtually all medical expenses, Norwegians pay very little directly toward health care. Although insurance is state controlled, each community elects its own health board and public health officer. State and local officials jointly run hospitals. The country has a shortage of nursing and retirement homes, in part because a higher percentage of Norwegians are living beyond age 75 than ever before.

Education

With free education through the university level, nearly everyone in Norway can read and write. The first ten years of schooling—for children aged six to sixteen—are compulsory. Based on principles of equal opportunities for all, the Norwegian school system decides on one elementary curriculum and method of teaching for the whole country. Schooling is divided into a four-year lower stage called *barnetrinnet,* for children aged 6 to 10, a three-year intermediate stage *(mellomtrinnet),* for children aged 10 to 13, and a three-year upper stage *(ungdomstrinnet)* from the age of 13. Classes focus on math, science, nature study, Christianity, Norwegian and foreign languages, physical training, and social studies.

When Norwegian high school students graduate, they participate in a tradition called *russ.* They dress up in red overalls and red berets and are allowed (indeed, encouraged) to partake in such mischief as unrestrained noise, removable graffiti, partying, and general obnoxiousness for several weeks.

Many students then continue with three years of upper secondary coursework. These students choose their own curriculum, including apprenticeships and vocational training. Students may opt to attend school away from their hometown. Starting in 1994, all Norwegians between the ages of 16 and 19 became entitled to upper secondary education.

A youth band prepares to perform in Trondheim's annual music festival called Saint Olaf's Days.

Norway boasts an enrollment rate of 100 percent for children ages 7 to 13, and a rate of 97 percent for children aged 16 to 19.

Norway has four universities—in Oslo, Bergen, Trondheim, and Tromsø—and several colleges, all of which are funded by the state. A network of regional colleges and technical and specialized institutions are part of the higher education system. In addition, laws require all cities and towns to have free public libraries, which the government partially supports. Nearly 15 percent of the government's annual budget goes toward education.

CULTURAL LIFE

Because Norwegians live in a land that is cold and dark for much of the year, and because the terrain is rugged, the people are generally hardy and self-reliant. Most love the challenges of the outdoors. Many Norwegians work outdoors, and almost all love to play there. In summer, the hills and lakes present excellent hiking, boating, and fishing opportunities. In winter, the mountains and forests provide downhill and cross-country skiing. Public access to wild land is guaranteed, and "Keep Out" or "No Trespassing" signs are rarely seen.

Norwegians also have a reputation for being self-sufficient when it comes to their homes and gardens. Tasks such as painting or fixing a fence are embraced with enthusiasm. Gardening is a special pleasure—a way to commune with the earth.

◉ Religion and Holidays

About 3.8 million people, or roughly 86 percent of Norwegians, belong to the Church of Norway, which is Evangelical Lutheran. The

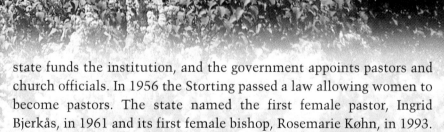

state funds the institution, and the government appoints pastors and church officials. In 1956 the Storting passed a law allowing women to become pastors. The state named the first female pastor, Ingrid Bjerkås, in 1961 and its first female bishop, Rosemarie Køhn, in 1993.

Many Norwegians who consider themselves Lutherans do not participate in weekly religious services. A majority are baptized, confirmed, married, and buried in religious ceremonies, but fewer than 20 percent of Norwegian adults attend church more than 5 times a year. The constitution guarantees complete religious freedom. The largest non-Lutheran religions in Norway are Islam, which claims about 50,000 members; Pentecostalism, which claims about 45,000; and Roman Catholicism, which claims about 42,600.

Stores and offices close in Norway on Christian holy days, such as Easter and Christmas. At Easter, many Norwegian families traditionally escape to cottages in the mountains for a week to enjoy the end of the skiing season.

Christmas baking is a special part of a family's preparations for the holiday in Norway.

Christmas is Norway's biggest annual festival. In addition to the religious significance of Christmas, the holiday falls during the shortest daylight hours of the year. Norwegians celebrated during this period long before Christianity arrived in the country. Ancient Norwegians believed that feasting soothed the powers of darkness and ensured a return of the sun.

In modern times, preparations for Christmas are made weeks in advance. At 5:00 P.M. on Christmas Eve, church bells toll, ringing in the holiday. After attending religious services, families join in a Christmas dinner and exchange gifts. The meal traditionally consists of roasted pork and sausage with sour cabbage or lutefisk—cod soaked in lye (a strong, salty liquor made from wood ashes). Christmas Day is typically a quiet time spent with family. On Boxing Day (the day after Christmas), a round of parties begins that lasts well into the new year.

National independence is celebrated on Constitution Day, May 17. This date is set aside even though Norway did not gain complete self-rule until nearly a century after it enacted its first constitution on May 17, 1814. In Oslo, men and women from all over the country show up for Constitution Day wearing the traditional *bunad*—an elaborate, regional folk costume. Each area of the country has its own decorations for the bunad.

Because summers in Norway are short, Norwegians celebrate Midsummer Eve, the brightest night of the year, which occurs in late June. People who own boats bring picnics out on the water to watch the night sun. At the first hint of dusk, Norwegians light bonfires along shorelines throughout the country.

Food

Living close to the sea, Norwegians historically have depended on fish and seafood for much of their diet. Cooks prepare fish in various ways, frequently serving it with boiled potatoes and vegetables at the main meal of the day—called *middag*—which most people eat between 4:00 and 6:00 P.M. Lingonberry jam, made from a tart, cranberry-like fruit, often accompanies middag.

Many of the fish dishes, such as fish balls and fish loaf, are very mild. Some of the national delicacies, however, are extremely salty and have a strong odor. Gravlaks, or cured salmon, is a favorite, and some Norwegians favor *rakørret*—trout that has been aged for several

LEFSE

A traditional Norwegian snack, *lefse* is a kind of soft, thin potato pancake that can be eaten plain or buttered. Many enjoy lefse with butter and sugar, while others like cinnamon or jelly.

3 cups boiling water	2 teaspoons white sugar
½ cup butter-flavored shortening	3 cups dry potato flakes
1 cup evaporated milk	3 cups all-purpose flour
1 teaspoon salt	

1. In a large bowl, mix together the boiling water, shortening, milk, salt, sugar, and potato flakes. Place in the refrigerator until thoroughly chilled (at least one hour).
2. After dough is chilled, add 3 cups of flour, using a pastry blender to cut in.
3. Divide dough into three equal-sized portions. Form into three logs. Chill thoroughly in the refrigerator.
4. Heat an electric griddle to 375°F (190°C).
5. Divide each log into eight pieces. Roll each piece to about the size of a 10-inch (25-centimeter) tortilla. Work additional flour into rounds as needed. Use care to press lightly with rolling pin when forming into rounds, as they are very tender. The weight of a large rolling pin is nearly enough.
6. Bake on the griddle until each round feels dry but not crisp. Turn frequently.
7. Cool on cloth. Cover with an additional cloth. Stack pieces on top of each other as they are baked. The steam will create a tenderer lefse. Recipe makes about 24 lefse.

months until it reaches a soft, buttery consistency with a slightly unpleasant smell. Mutton, or sheep, is the most common meat, and blood sausage (a spicy mixture of livestock's blood and flour) is a national specialty.

Norwegians eat three other meals a day—breakfast, lunch, and supper. Each of these meals features *smørbrød*, or open-faced sandwiches. Smørbrød consist of bread or crackers layered with various combinations of cheese, jam, salmon spread, boiled egg, tomato, cucumber, sausage, herring, and sardines. Traditional desserts include fruit soup, *risengryngrøt* (rice pudding, a Christmas treat), and fresh berries during the summer. Coffee is perhaps the national drink in Norway, and guests usually are served coffee with cakes or smørbrød.

Language

Norwegian is part of the Germanic family of languages and draws from many European sources. Because mountains and fjords historically isolated Norwegian settlements from one another, numerous dialects exist in Norway.

Two forms of the Norwegian language—*bokmål* (standard Norwegian) and *nynorsk* (new Norwegian)—are used officially and are very closely related. Bokmål developed during Norway's four-hundred-year union with Denmark and is spoken in large towns, which were influenced strongly by Danish rule. Although spoken bokmål sounds very different from Danish, the written form is nearly identical to Danish. Created in reaction to Danish rule, nynorsk dates from the mid-1800s. This form combines elements from the major rural dialects to produce a more distinctly Norwegian language.

In recent years, some Norwegian language experts have sought to streamline the two official tongues into one, called *samnorsk* (common Norwegian). The combined form would simplify communication between urban and rural areas and in the mass media, which now alternates between the two forms. Some Norwegians, however, feel strongly that bokmål and nynorsk—as well as the many dialects that influenced them—are part of the Norwegian heritage and should not be allowed to die out.

Literature

Norwegian literature can be divided into three historical periods. Old Norse (Norwegian-Icelandic) poems and legends originated in the Viking Age. Danish rule in Norway from about 1400 to 1814 heavily influenced writing styles referred to as Norwegian-Danish literature. Liberation from Denmark in 1814 marks the beginning of the modern period, with nationalist works shaped by Norwegian concerns.

A good **storyteller** *(right)* was a welcome guest in any Viking camp. For links to Norwegian folktales, myths, and legends, go to vgsbooks.com.

During the Old Norse period, Norwegian Vikings who settled in Iceland transmitted their beliefs, history, and myths through storytelling. In the thirteenth century, Norse tales began to appear in Icelandic manuscripts. The oldest known collection of poems is the *Poetic Edda*, which tells of the mythical gods, goddesses, heroes, and heroines of Scandinavia. Later Norse literature includes sagas, or prose epics, told by Icelanders. *Heimskringla*, a saga by Snorri Sturluson, chronicles the lives of Norwegian kings in the thirteenth century.

During the first two centuries of Danish rule, writing in Norwegian nearly ceased. Norwegian authors adopted Danish when it became the official language of Norway. By the eighteenth century, Norwegian writers were contributing significantly to Danish literature. Playwright Ludvig Holberg spent most of his life in Denmark and was the most distinguished author of the 1700s. His comedies are still performed on stages in Norway and Denmark.

When Norway was transferred from Danish to Swedish control in 1814, a strong nationalist movement arose. Henrik Wergeland, who led the fight against Danish tradition, is considered the founder of Norwegian literature. Nationalism spurred an interest in writing down oral literature, which had existed among peasants for centuries. These folktales were imaginative stories that often began with the phrase, "Once upon a time." The proliferation of folktales all over the world is evidence that this is one of the oldest forms of literature. Despite its old roots, however, folktales were not written down in Norway until the nineteenth century, because they were held in low esteem by the educated classes. Peter Asbjørnsen and Jørgen Moe were the first Norwegians to gather and publish folktales, beginning in the 1840s.

In the second half of the nineteenth century, writers turned to realism (realistic representation without idealism) and social criticism. Bjørnstjerne Bjørnson, Henrik Ibsen, Jonas Lie, and Alexander Kielland stood out among others in this new generation and became known as the Big Four. The dramatist Henrik Ibsen gained world fame for masterpieces such as *Peer Gynt, A Doll's House,* and *The Master Builder,* which probe human aspirations and limitations. The novels, plays, and poems of Bjørnson, who was also a political and social leader, earned him a Nobel Prize for literature in 1903. Camilla Collett wrote Norway's first feminist novel, *The Governor's Daughter,* in 1855, decrying the position of women forced into marriage.

Henrik Ibsen

Around the turn of the twentieth century, writers became concerned with the struggles of the individual, which were often expressed in lyric poetry. The novels of Knut Hamsun—such as *Hunger* and *Growth of the Soil*—explore social problems and portray people who reject modern society. Hamsun was awarded a Nobel Prize in 1920. In 1928 Sigrid Undset also won a Nobel Prize. She is best known for her historical novels, especially the trilogy *Kristin Lavransdatter,* which is set in fourteenth-century Norway.

Sigrid Undset

Contemporary Norwegian literature has been characterized as chaotic and fantastical. A growing number of authors' books are sent abroad each year for translation—and often find foreign sales successful. For example, in 1991 the Norwegian teacher Jostein Gaarder published *Sophie's World,* a story that begins when fourteen-year-old Sophie receives a strange letter with one sentence: "Who are you?" As one thing leads to another, Sophie develops a strong thirst for knowledge and learns about the ideas of European philosophers. To date, *Sophie's World* has been published in forty-four languages and has sold more than fifteen million copies throughout the world.

Visual Arts

Among the oldest artistic works in Norway are Viking wood carvings. The Vikings decorated ships, buildings, wagons, sleighs, and other objects with intricate carvings of animals—especially dragons, horses, snakes, and swans. Floral and geometric patterns were also popular designs. Most of the Viking artifacts have been found at burial sites.

When the nationalist movement arose in literature in the nineteenth century, the visual arts also changed.

ROSEMALING

The Norwegian art of decorative painting on flat wood surfaces, or rosemaling, is a rustic tradition. Flowery designs and tendril motifs are strong themes, but actual rose designs are not very common. The oldest surviving examples date from about 1700, though some historians believe it is a much older tradition than that.

The decorative motifs typical of Norwegian rosemaling vary from district to district and include adapted Swedish, German, Dutch, and French elements. To see more examples of rosemaling, visit vgsbooks.com for links.

Paintings of Norwegian landscapes and depictions of daily life became popular. Johan Christian Dahl led the development of a Norwegian style in painting. He also introduced the mountain as a symbol that would recur in the works of later Norwegian artists and writers. Adolph Tidemand and Hans Gude followed in the nationalist footsteps of Dahl.

In the late 1800s, Frits Thaulow, Christian Krohg, and Erik Werenskiold painted realistic images of Norway and its people. Edvard Munch, one of Norway's greatest painters, also began working during this period, but he soon rejected the detailed realism of his contemporaries. Instead Munch pioneered the Norwegian Expressionist movement, which uses objects and events to arouse inner emotions. His most famous works—including *The Scream*, *The Sick Child*, *The Vampire*, and *In Hell, Self-Portrait*—depict individuals who are tormented and isolated.

Norwegian Expressionist painter Edvard Munch is best known for portraits such as *Self-Portrait with Spanish Influenza (above)*. He left his personal papers and paintings to the city of Oslo when he died.

Gustav Vigeland, a sculptor and a contemporary of Munch, also used Expressionism. Frogner Park in Oslo contains about 150 of his massive symbolic figures representing various aspects and stages of life. Contemporary Norwegian art includes the work of the sculptor Bard Breivik, whose sculptures examine the relationships between humans and their tools, and the output of the many artists working with computers.

▶ Architecture

Because of Norway's vast forests, wood has been a major element of the country's architectural designs. Working with wood is also easier—and cheaper—than working with stone, so peasants, farmers, and other people have always enjoyed wooden homes. Members of the wealthier classes were more inclined to display their wealth by crafting massive stone homes.

Most religious buildings were also made of stone, but by the twelfth century the wooden stave church became a major art form.

Located in Lærdal, the **Borgund stave church** was built in the twelfth century without any metal nails or bolts. Visit vgsbooks.com for links that will help you learn more about Norway's unique stave churches.

Twenty-nine of the original nine hundred stave churches survive, and they are among the oldest wooden buildings in the world. Named for their vertical supporting posts, these churches are distinguished by detailed carved designs and dragon-headed gables resembling the prows of Viking ships. The designs combine Christian and Viking influences. Constructed on stone foundations to prevent moisture in the ground from rotting the wood, stave churches used no nails.

Sports and Recreation

Outdoor activities are an important part of Norwegian life. Many Norwegians are nature enthusiasts and have easy access to recreational areas. Hiking in the mountains or on wooded hillsides is a favorite activity. In the winter, Norwegians ski across snow-covered wildernesses. On some trails, people can ski or walk for days, spending nights in cabins located at regular intervals along the way.

Skiing is the country's national sport, and it may have originated in Norway thousands of years ago as a means of transport. Four kinds of skiing—alpine (slalom and downhill racing), cross-country, ski jumping, and biathlon (which combines cross-country and rifle shooting)—are popular. One in three Norwegians skis competitively. Ice-skating is also a favorite winter sport, and some people play bandy, a form of hockey. Competitive skiing and speed skating appear on television.

In 2001 Norwegian explorer Liv Arnesen and her American partner Ann Bancroft became the first women to ski across Antarctica, each of them pulling a 250-pound (114-kilogram) sled. Both are former schoolteachers, and thousands of schoolchildren tracked their 2,300-mile (3,700-km) journey, which lasted about one hundred days.

Norway has won more Winter Olympic medals than any other country, besides the former Soviet Union, and winter sports stars are much beloved. Figure skater Sonja Henie went into history as the Queen of the Ice, winning Olympic gold medals in figure skating in 1928, 1932, and 1936, nine world championships, and six European championships. Henie introduced ballet moves to the sport, transforming it into an artistic exhibition. The cross-country skier Bjørn Dæhlie is known as the best cross-country skier ever. At the Nagano Olympics in 1998, he picked up three gold medals. He has claimed eight career Olympic golds, the most by any individual in history, and twelve Olympic medals overall.

The Norwegian skier **Kjetil Andre Aamodt** took two gold medals in the 2002 Winter Olympics in Salt Lake City, Utah.

Soccer is the nation's main summer sport, and it attracts thousands of spectators each season. In 2000 the Norwegian women's soccer team won the Olympic gold medal, with a dramatic 3–2 victory over the defending champions, the United States. Other fair-weather activities include boating, fishing, rowing, swimming, and cycling.

THE ECONOMY

Due to its relatively low population, Norway's economy is small compared to that of most European nations. Still, Norwegians are considered among the most prosperous people in the world. Two factors—the development of hydroelectric power since 1900 and the discovery of oil in the 1960s—have aided economic expansion. If the gross national income (GNI) were divided equally among all the nation's citizens in 2000, each person would have received about $36,000—one of the highest GNIs per capita in western Europe.

However, some economists—and many Norwegian voters—suggest that exorbitant taxes and high prices of goods actually give Norwegians a lower standard of living than other countries with lower GNIs per capita. Norwegians have a deep-seated desire for fairness and equality, a sentiment that is evident in their strong welfare state. But equal treatment for all is an expensive proposition. More than half the government's budget goes to finance social services, and additional money goes to build roads, schools, hospitals, and other infrastructure.

Income is taxed at a rate ranging from one-third to two-thirds and continues to rise, yet Norwegians increasingly criticize the quality of the services gained from those taxes. The government has also been reprimanded for allowing an influx of immigrants in recent years, another perceived burden on the welfare state.

Oil

In 1969 Phillips Petroleum, a U.S. company, discovered the Ekofisk oil fields off Norway's North Sea coast. By 1975 Norway was exporting oil products, which greatly boosted the economy. In 1986 revenues from oil amounted to nearly 20 percent of the GNI.

However, by the end of the twentieth century, the oil and gas markets had changed radically. Competition was greater than ever, and prices had gone down. In 2000 oil accounted for only about 15 percent of Norway's GNI. Nevertheless, Norway remains one of the world's largest exporters of oil, and it anticipates tapping considerable offshore reserves above the Arctic Circle. The government is also exploring for oil in the Barents Sea.

After the discovery of oil, the Storting voted to limit annual production to conserve the oil fields. In 1972 the government created a company named Statoil to oversee all aspects of the industry, from exploration and drilling to transport, processing, and selling of oil and natural gas. In June 2001, Norway's government privatized part of Statoil, putting almost 18 percent of the company up for sale on the Norwegian and American stock exchanges. The move is expected to make Statoil more efficient.

Services

In addition to the valuable employment opportunities provided by Norway's massive government services, many private services—such as real estate, business, and insurance—provide essential income for Norwegians. Services also include the transportation, tourism, and trade industries.

Although Norway's rugged terrain makes building roads and railroads difficult and expensive, the nation has developed a diverse and efficient system of transportation. A network of roads, railways, and water routes serves the country. Most Norwegian households have a car, but public transit is well developed. Express buses link the biggest towns. The opening of the first rail line in 1854 signaled the beginning of increased mobility within Norway. In modern times, approximately

While laying and maintaining railroad tracks in Norway's mountainous terrain is expensive, electricity to keep the **trains** moving is not, thanks to Norway's development of hydropower.

two-thirds of the nation's tracks run on electricity. With more than forty airports, Norway also relies increasingly on airways to cover the vast, mountainous distances within the country. For centuries, water transit was the most effective means of transportation in Norway. In modern times, ferryboats provide a vital link between motor routes that stop at the edge of the fjords. Vessels also travel the coastline.

Partly due to improving transportation, Norway has seen tourism grow in spite of its high prices. In winter, skiers head for the mountains, and in summer many Europeans take trips to Oslo, Bergen, and Stavanger. Norway's beautiful and varied terrain provides visitors with much to see and do.

Norway has a long history as a trading nation. A shortage of natural resources forced early Norwegians to exchange fish and timber for other goods from foreign lands. The country depends on international trade for much of its prosperity. Norway's merchant fleet is among the world's largest shipping lines.

A ferry *(upper left)* docks in Oslo harbor. A container ship *(lower right)* delivers containers of goods for trucks to haul inland.

Norway's export trade changed dramatically in the 1970s with the development of oil and natural gas reserves in the North Sea. These two products account for nearly half of all goods sold abroad. Other major exports include machinery, ships, aluminum, chemicals, pulp and paper products, and food items. Imports include machinery, transportation equipment, petroleum products, chemicals, foodstuffs, and ores. Norway trades most heavily with Great Britain, Sweden, and Germany. The United States, Denmark, and France are also important trading partners.

Industry

Because Norway lacks large reserves of coal to fuel factories, it developed industries later than many other European countries. After the nation began to harness hydropower from its rivers, however, it had a cheap source of electricity, spurring rapid industrialization in the twentieth century. Early industries in Norway depended on local raw materials, such as iron ore, timber, and fish. Since the discovery of oil in 1969, a petrochemical industry has also arisen.

About half the nation's factories are located near Oslo. In the early 1970s, manufacturing contributed nearly 30 percent to Norway's GNI. But wage increases and economic conditions made Norwegian products more expensive and therefore less competitive on the international market. As a result, manufacturing in the early twenty-first century contributed only 14 percent to Norway's GNI.

Factories, such as this lumber and iron pellet factory in Kirkenes, get raw materials from abroad.

Visit vgsbooks.com for links to websites with information about Norway's economy, to see a currency converter for the most up-to-date exchange rate so you can learn how many kroner are in a U.S. dollar, and for information on Norwegian fishing, including whaling.

The most important manufactured products are oil products, chemical products, metals such as aluminum and magnesium, processed foods, and wood pulp and paper. Aluminum is a metal produced from bauxite, and Norway is an important aluminum-producing country. Norway imports most of the raw materials it refines, such as bauxite, and then exports them immediately after refining. After Canada, Norway is the largest exporter of metal in the world.

Hydroelectricity remains the principal source of power in Norway. Ninety-nine percent of Norway's installed electric energy is produced by hydroelectric power schemes. It is the only self-sufficient country in Europe, easily meeting its domestic energy needs, and it has been exporting hydroelectricity since 1993.

Although the shipbuilding industry has declined since the 1970s, Norway remains a leading shipping nation. Some shipbuilding companies have shifted their production to oil rigs and other equipment for the North Sea oil fields.

Agriculture, Forestry, and Fishing

Until the twentieth century, agriculture was a mainstay of the Norwegian economy and the most important source of employment. In modern times, however, agriculture employs relatively few Norwegians, accounting for only about 3 percent of the GNI. The most important branch of the agricultural sector is livestock raising.

Although most Norwegians work in the manufacturing, oil, or service sectors of the economy, agricultural output has increased in the last cen-

Sheep in mountain pasture

tury. The growth is due to mechanized equipment, fertilizers, improved animal feed and breeding techniques, and education. Furthermore, government funding and cooperative organizations—in which groups of farmers can buy equipment and sell goods collectively—have eased the financial burdens that once plagued agricultural workers.

The government oversees the welfare of farming to ensure its continuation. The nation's rugged terrain leaves only 3 percent of the land suitable for cultivation. Nevertheless, Norwegians place a priority on being as self-sufficient in food as possible. Consequently, agriculture manages to provide about half of the nation's foodstuffs, and Norway buys the rest from other countries. Although government assistance is extensive, most farmers own their land and work relatively small plots that average about 25 acres (10 hectares).

Livestock raising and dairy farming are concentrated in Vestlandet. The broad valleys of Øslandet and Trøndelag are best suited for crops. Food crops include potatoes, fruits, and vegetables. The supply of meat and dairy products meets domestic demand, but Norway must import fruits and vegetables in addition to grain.

Terracing on Norwegian farms allows farmers to cultivate as much land as possible.

Commercial logging is limited by government regulation in Norway.

To supplement their incomes, some Norwegian farmers also engage in commercial forestry. Land owned by farmers contains half the nation's productive forests, which are located primarily in the counties of Nord-Trøndelag, Hedmark, Oppland, and Buskerud.

Most of the timber is softwood—including birch, pine, and spruce—and is used in wood processing. Logging could not be increased without using up the forests, which government regulations protect. As a result, the nation imports timber from Sweden and Finland to keep its processing plants operating at full capacity.

Norway has a long history as a fishing nation. Although this activity earns less than 1 percent of the yearly GNI, Norway ranks as one of the world's leading fishing countries. Fishing provides almost 9 percent of the nation's total export revenue.

The number of anglers registered in Norway has dropped by more than half since the 1960s. Nevertheless, the size of the catch has increased because more crews work year-round at only one occupation. Furthermore, bigger vessels and more effective equipment enable crews to take in larger hauls in less time.

Racks of codfish drying, such as these near Henningsvaer, are a common sight in the northwest. Dried cod is the main ingredient of lutefisk. Some cod is later smoked, which is also popular.

Fish farming of salmon and trout in the fjords and inlets along the coast has also become an important industry. In the 1980s, the export value of salmon and trout surpassed that of cod. Most of Norway's hatcheries are located in the counties of Hordaland, Møre og Romsdal, and Sør-Trøndelag.

Some types of marine life once caught by Norwegian anglers are in danger of extinction. To promote the continued existence of these species, the government either forbids or strictly regulates the catches. For example, quotas restrict the size of hauls of herring, and anglers have largely replaced herring with capelin. Once a renowned whaling nation, Norway temporarily ceased commercial whaling to allow these mammals to replenish their numbers. Commercial whaling was resumed in 1993, however, against bans set by the International Whaling Commission. In 2000 Norway and Japan appealed to the United Nations to overturn its ban on the commercial trade in minke whales—a species the two countries claim is well-stocked—but were refused. Each whaling season, Norwegian police go on the alert to protect whalers from protests by animal welfare activists.

> Norway lifted its ban on hunting minke whales in 1993, but international trade of whale products, such as blubber, which is a delicacy in Japan, is forbidden. Japan and Norway argued for lifting the trade ban at a convention of the United Nations in 2000, but it was voted down. Norway continues to hunt and collect blubber, though, and by 2001, hunters had more than eight hundred tons (726 metric tons) of blubber stocked up, waiting for the chance to sell. Whale blubber commands a very high price on the international market.

◉ The Future

Norway, as an isolated and rugged land, has produced a people who are independent and adventurous. But Norwegians also believe that all people deserve help, a belief that may also stem from living in an often harsh environment. In the near future, in the face of soaring taxes and wavering oil prices, the people of Norway will have to find new ways to reconcile their social-welfare demands with an increasingly volatile economic climate.

The dilemma extends to Norway's international role, as well. After hundreds of years of rule by Sweden and Denmark and occupation by the Nazis during World War II, Norwegians generally believe it is best to stand alone. Norway is the only nation to have voted on and rejected joining the European Union twice, even though neighboring countries—Sweden and Finland—have recently joined. But its recent humanitarian foreign policy, as evidenced by its role in the Oslo Agreement, can be seen as an attempt to share the social ideals found in Norwegian domestic culture. The partial privatization of Statoil is another sign of Norway's assimilation into the international economic community.

Many people expect the issue of the EU to come up again, with perhaps another vote in the near future. But if Norway joins, it will only do so when joining is in the best interest of all Norwegians. Regardless of what happens, Norway's challenge in the coming decades will be to balance the high price of their social ideals with their changing economy.

SOCIAL WELFARE AND TAXES

About 35 percent of Norway's budget is spent on its health and social welfare system. While Norwegians certainly appreciate their government-granted right to economic assistance and other forms of community support during illness, old age, or unemployment, many resent the exorbitant taxes they must pay to finance this system. Particularly frustrating is the fact that social security payments have increased even as population growth remains minimal. More than 9 percent of Norway's working population in 2000 subsisted partly or wholly on disability benefits, a number that had doubled over the previous twenty years. But the outlook is not totally bleak. After the number of social welfare recipients tripled during the 1980s, it stabilized during the 1990s and has begun to decline.

10,000 B.C.	The earliest-known humans live in Norway.
3000 B.C.	Norwegians establish permanent communities.
A.D. 600	Popluation begins to increase rapidly, leading to a shortage of farmland. Vikings explore the seas and surrounding lands.
C. 800	The earliest-known written communication in Norway appears.
C. 880-933	Reign of Harald Fairhair (Harald I), first to rule a unified Norway
982	Erik the Red sails to Greenland.
C. 995-1000	Reign of Olaf Tryggvason (Olaf I), a great-grandson of Harald I. Olaf I tries to force Christianity on the people and is killed in a naval battle with a union of Danish, Swedish, and dissatisfied Norwegian forces.
C. 1000	Leif Eriksson, son of Erik the Red, sails to the eastern coast of North America, establishing the first European colony on North America.
1015	Olaf Haraldsson (Olaf II) reunites Norway and makes himself king. Olaf II continues to force Christianity upon Norwegians.
1030	Olaf II is killed. Norway falls under Danish control.
1130-1240	Civil wars ravage the country.
1240	Haakon Haakonsson (Haakon IV) restores lasting peace and later a new law restricts succession to the throne to the oldest legitimate son of a king.
1319	Magnus Eriksson (Magnus VII) becomes king of Norway and Sweden.
1349-1350	Bubonic plague kills at least half of the population of Norway.
1380	Haakon VI dies and his wife, Margaret, who is the ruler of Denmark, becomes the queen of Norway as well.
1397	Margaret formally unites Norway, Denmark, and Sweden in the Union of Kalmar.
1523	Sweden breaks away from the Union of Kalmar.
1536	Denmark dissolves the Norwegian national council, stripping the country of its voice in Norwegian affairs. Denmark makes Lutheranism the official religion of Norway.
1624	Oslo burns and is later rebuilt under the name Christiania.
1804-1814	Many Norwegians starve during the Napoleonic Wars.
1811	University of Oslo is established.
1814	Through the Treaty of Kiel, Sweden takes over control of Norway from Denmark. Norway resists Swedish control, and on May 17 it declares independence and drafts its own constitution. However, Sweden defeats Norwegian troops, and in November King Charles XIII of Sweden becomes Norway's ruler.
1829	Henrik Wergeland publishes *Digte*, beginning his career as a champion of Norwegian nationalism in literature.
1855	Camilla Collett writes *The Governor's Daughter*, Norway's first feminist novel.

1866   Henrik Ibsen achieves his first success with the
        play *Brand*.

1866-1915   More than 600,000 Norwegians emigrate to North America
            in search of jobs and farmland.

1903   Bjørnstjerne Bjørnson becomes the first Norwegian to win the
        Nobel Prize for literature.

1905   Sweden agrees to recognize Norway's independence. Prince Charles
        of Denmark becomes the Norwegian king, under the name Haakon VII.

1913   Norwegian women gain suffrage rights.

1914-1918   Norway, along with Sweden and Denmark, remains neutral during World
            War I.

1928   Sonja Henie wins her first of nine career gold medals in figure skating.

1929   Worldwide economic depression spikes Norway's unemployment rate.

1939   World War II begins. Norway again remains neutral.

1940   Nazi forces invade on April 9. After two months of fighting, Norway surrenders.

1945   German forces in Norway surrender on May 8. Norway joins the United Nations
        (UN), and Norwegian Trygve Lie becomes the UN's first secretary-general.

1949   Norway joins the North Atlantic Treaty Organization (NATO).

1952   Oslo, Norway, hosts the Winter Olympic Games.

1957   King Haakon VII dies and King Olav V comes to the throne.

1959   Norway and six other countries form an economic union called the European
        Free Trade Association (EFTA).

1961   The first female pastor, Ingrid Bjerkås, is appointed in the Church of Norway.

1962   The country's first national park is created in the mountains of Rondane.

1966   The Storting passes the National Insurance Act.

1969   Oil is discovered in the North Sea off Norway's coast.

1972   Statoil is created to control all aspects of the oil industry in Norway.

1981   Gro Harlem Brundtland becomes Norway's first female prime minister.

1991   King Olav V dies, and King Harald V assumes the throne. The Labor Party forms
        its third minority government with Gro Harlem Brundtland as prime minister.

1993   Norway helps forge the Oslo Agreement between Israel and the Palestine
        Liberation Organization. Norway resumes hunting minke whales after a
        seven-year international moratorium. The first woman bishop is ordained.

1994   Voters reject membership in the European Union. Lillehammer hosts the
        seventeenth Winter Olympics.

1995   The Troll platform (oil rig) is towed out into the North Sea. It is the
        tallest cement structure in the world.

1998   The price of oil drops dramatically due to overproduction, contribut-
        ing to a decrease in the value of the Norwegian krone.

2000   Norwegian Olympic women's soccer team wins the gold medal.

2001   Statoil becomes partially privatized. Shake-up election forces
        fourth change of government since 1996.

2002   Skier Kjetil Andre Aamodt wins two of Norway's eleven gold
        medals in the Winter Olympics in Salt Lake City, Utah.

NAME The Kingdom of Norway

AREA 125,050 square miles (323,880 square kilometers)

MAIN LANDFORMS Langfjella, Jostedalsbreen, Hardangervidda, Finnmarksvidda, Lofoten Archipelago, Vesterålen Archipelago

HIGHEST POINT Galdhøpiggen (8,100 ft.; 2,469 m above sea level)

LOWEST POINT Sea level

MAJOR RIVERS Glåma River, Alteelva River, Tana River, Orkla River, Namsen River, Lågen River, Otra River

ANIMALS Cod, deer, elk, foxes, fulmars, gannets, grayling, gulls, herring, lemmings, mackerel, marten, otters, perch, pike, polar foxes, polar hare, puffins, reindeer, salmon, trout, wolverines, wolves

CAPITAL CITY Oslo

OTHER MAJOR CITIES Bergen, Bodø, Drammen, Kristiansund, Skien, Stavanger, Tromsø, Trondheim

OFFICIAL LANGUAGE Norwegian (nynorsk and bokmål)

MONETARY UNIT Kroner. 100 øre = 1 krone.

NORWEGIAN CURRENCY

The first Norwegian coin was made around the year 1000 and has little relation to modern Norwegian coins. The Royal Norwegian Mint was created in 1628 and was moved in 1686 to the city of Kongsberg, where it is still located. Modern Norwegian currency dates back to 1875, when the Money Act determined that the monetary unit would be the krone, divided into 100 øre. Banknotes are available in denominations of 50, 100, 200, 500, and 1,000 kroner. Coins are minted in denominations of 50 øre and 1, 5, 10, and 20 kroner.

Fast Facts

Currency

Ruled by Denmark until 1814, Norway flew Denmark's flag—red with a white cross. The current flag was created in 1821, during the period when Norway was ruled by Sweden. The flag maintained the red field with a white cross and added a blue cross on top of the white. These three colors—red, white, and blue—were chosen in honor of the French tricolor, a symbol of revolution and liberty.

The Norwegian national anthem started out as a poem, written by the dramatist and poet Bjørnstjerne Bjørnson, called "Yes, We Love This Land." The composer Rikard Nordraak wrote music to the poem, and the song was adopted as Norway's national anthem in 1864, when the first public recital was given on the fiftieth anniversary of the Norwegian constitution. This translation is by O. O. Lien.

Yes, We Love This Land
Yes we love this land of ours
As with mountain domes,
Stormlash'd o'er the sea it towers
With the thousand homes.
Love it dearly, ever thinking
Of our fathers' strife
And the land of Saga sinking
Dreams upon our life.

Norsemen in whatever station
Thank our mighty God;
He has kindly saved our nation
From oppression's rod.
That for which our sires contended
And our mothers wailed
Silently the Lord defended
So our rights prevailed.

For a link to an opportunity to listen to Norway's national anthem, "Yes, We Love This Land," go to vgsbooks.com.

GRO HARLEM BRUNDTLAND (b. 1939) Born in Oslo, Brundtland became prime minister for the first time in 1981. She was the youngest person and the first woman ever to hold the office of prime minister in Norway. With two other periods as prime minister (1986–1989 and 1990–1996), Brundtland was head of government for more than ten years. She became director-general of the World Health Organization in 1998, where her many skills as doctor, politician, activist, and manager have come together.

JOHAN CHRISTIAN DAHL (1788–1857) Dahl was born in Bergen. As a painter, he was a leader in establishing a Norwegian nationalistic style in painting. He established the mountain as a popular symbol in Norwegian paintings.

BJØRN DÆHLIE (b. 1967) Dæhlie is a cross-country skier who has won twelve medals at the Winter Olympics, the most of any athlete in history. His eight gold medals are also a Winter Olympics record and have put him one behind the all-time record for the Winter and Summer Games. Dæhlie also has been successful in non-Olympic competition, winning six World Cup titles and nine gold medals at the World Championships. He was born in Råholt.

EDVARD GRIEG (1843–1907) Born in Bergen, Grieg was a world-famous composer who was best-known for writing the music for Henrik Ibsen's play *Peer Gynt*. He wrote piano sonatas, choral music, and folk songs. He was also known by many Norwegians for carrying a rubber frog in his pocket.

KNUT HAMSUN (1859–1952) A novelist best known for his novels *Hunger* and *Growth of the Soil*, Hamsun was awarded the Nobel Prize for literature in 1920. He lived in the United States for several years in the 1880s and worked as a streetcar operator and farmer. He was born in Lom.

SONJA HENIE (1912–1969) Henie was a figure skater who is known for introducing ballet moves to the sport, transforming it into dramatic exhibition. She won Olympic gold medals in 1928, 1932, and 1936, nine world championships, and six European championships. Her victory in 1927 at the World Figure Skating Championship in Oslo was tainted by controversy because all three Norwegian judges voted for her, while the Austrian and German judges gave higher scores to her competitor, Herma Planck-Szabo, of Austria. After that, no country had more than one judge on the panel. She was born in Oslo.

THOR HEYERDAHL (1914–2002) Considered by many to be the best-known explorer of the twentieth century, Heyerdahl was more interested in anthropology than exploring uncharted territories. In 1947 he built a raft in the style of the Incas and sailed from Peru to Polynesia to prove that it was possible for early South Americans to have done so. He was born in Larvik.

HENRIK IBSEN (1828–1906) Born in Skien, Ibsen was a playwright whose plays revolutionized theater with their realism. He was also known for his support of women's rights and for creating strong female characters, such as Nora in *A Doll's House.*

LEIF ERIKSSON In approximately A.D. 1000, this Viking explorer landed on the eastern coast of North America. Eriksson called the territory Vinland and established a settlement on what would become the Canadian island of Newfoundland. He was the son of another famous Viking explorer, Erik Thorvaldson (Erik the Red).

EDVARD MUNCH (1863–1944) Munch was a painter known for portraying the trauma of modern life. As a forerunner of Expressionism, he was one of the world's most influential modern artists. He is best known for his painting *The Scream.* He was a born in Løten.

FRIDTJOF NANSEN (1861–1930) Nansen was an explorer, zoologist, and statesman who won the Nobel Peace Prize in 1922 for his role in saving more than seven million refugees of the Russian Revolution from starvation and disease. In 1893 he headed an expedition to reach the North Pole by fastening his vessel to an ice floe and drifting with it. He reached 86°14' North, then the highest latitude reached by humans. He was born in Kristiania (later called Oslo).

VIDKUN QUISLING (1887–1945) Quisling was a military officer and politician who actively collaborated with the Nazis during the German conquest of Norway in World War II. After the war, he was found guilty of high treason and executed. He was born in Fyresdal.

LIV ULLMANN (b. 1939) Ullmann is a popular and talented Norwegian actress who chose to make her career starring in Swedish films—such as *The Serpent's Egg* and other films directed by Ingmar Bergman—because she felt that the Swedish are far less inhibited about social issues in art than the Norwegians. Ullmann is also an accomplished film director. She was born in Japan, where her father worked briefly as an engineer.

SIGRID UNDSET (1882–1949) Undset was awarded the Nobel Prize for literature in 1928 for her trilogy of historical novels *Kristin Lavransdatter,* set in fourteenth-century Norway. She was born to parents of Norwegian ancestry in Kalundborg, Denmark, and educated in Kristiania.

GUSTAV VIGELAND (1869–1943) Born in Mandal, Vigeland was the first Norwegian sculptor to win international fame. An entire park in Oslo is dedicated to him and contains more than fifty of his sculptures. His best-known sculptures include *The Monolith* and *Angry Boy.*

ALTA MUSEUM Visitors to the Alta Museum, just southwest of the town of Alta, can see four groupings of prehistoric rock carvings featuring ships, reindeer, and a man with a bow and arrow. The petroglyphs were discovered in 1973 and date from 2,500 to 6,000 years ago.

BRYGGEN This World Heritage Site is a row of fourteenth-century painted wooden buildings facing a harbor in Bergen. It is regarded as one of the most charming walks in all of Europe.

FREDRIKSTAD Norway's oldest fortified city, Fredrikstad lies at the mouth of the Glåma, Norway's longest river. Its bastions and moat date to the seventeenth century, and its Old Town has been preserved and has museums, artisan workshops, antique shops, and bookstores.

FROGNER PARK This park in Oslo contains more than fifty copper statues by the sculptor Gustav Vigeland. The highlight of the park is *The Monolith*, a 470-ton (426-metric-ton) sculpture that depicts hundreds of people scrambling to a peak.

GEIRANGER FJORD Perhaps the most dramatic fjord in Norway, this 10-mile-long (16-km) fjord is best known for its waterfalls—the Seven Sisters, the Bridal Veil, and the Suitor.

KARL JOHANS GATE Karl Johans gate is a pedestrian-only street that serves as the hub of Oslo, running between the Royal Palace and the central railway station. The street is lined with stores, cafés, and clubs, and attracts people almost twenty-four hours a day.

KRISTIANSAND DYREPARK One of the most popular spots in Norway, this park, located in Kristiansand, is actually five separate parks—a water park, a forested park, an entertainment park, a fairy-tale park, and a zoo. The fairy-tale park, Cardamom Town, brings to life a book by Norwegian illustrator and writer Thorbjørn Egner.

THE NATIONAL GALLERY The National Gallery is Norway's official art museum, located in downtown Oslo. Many Scandinavian impressionists are represented here, including Norwegians Christian Krohg, Johan Christian Dahl, and Edvard Munch.

OLYMPIC PARK Olympic Park in Lillehammer was the location of the opening and closing ceremonies at the 1994 Winter Olympics. The park contains a ski-jumping arena and a tower from which visitors can see the entire town.

THE ROYAL PALACE Built in 1848, the palace is closed to visitors, but the garden is open. An equestrian statue of Karl Johan, king of Sweden and Norway from 1818 to 1844, stands in the square in front of the palace. The palace is located in Oslo.

bunad: the traditional folk costume of Norway. The appearance varies from region to region.

Expressionism: a movement in art and literature in which artists depict objects and events to try to elicit in the viewer the emotions that the objects and events arouse in the artist

fjord: created by glaciers, a narrow inlet of the sea between cliffs or steep slopes

folktale: a usually anonymous, timeless, placeless, and very imaginative tale circulated orally among a people. Norwegian folktales existed among peasants for centuries, and often began with the phrase, "Once upon a time."

Lutheranism: a Protestant religion developed by a German man named Martin Luther in the first half of the sixteenth century. Lutheranism is Norway's national religion.

midnight sun: the sun above the horizon at midnight in the Arctic or Antarctic summer. The phenomenon occurs from mid-May through July in far northern Norway.

nationalism: loyalty and devotion to a nation, often to the point where people hold their own nation's culture and interests as more important than those of other nations

North Atlantic Current: a current in the Atlantic Ocean related to the Gulf Stream Current, which originates in the Caribbean Sea where the waters are warmed by the hot Caribbean sun. In winter, the Gulf Stream warms the cold westerly winds that blow toward Europe, and these gusts, in turn, make coastal regions of Norway as much as 45°F (25°C) warmer in January than the world average for the same latitude.

ombudsman: a government official appointed to receive and investigate complaints made by individuals against public officials

realism: a movement in art and literature characterized by a dedication to real life or to nature and to accurate representation without idealism

social welfare: an organized program of public services designed to promote the well-being of all humans in a society, especially people who are disadvantaged because they are sick, destitute, or otherwise unfortunate

stave church: wooden churches distinguished by construction from vertical pieces of wood rather than horizontal pieces. Detailed carved designs and dragon-headed gables resembling the prows of Viking ships also make these churches distinctive. The designs combine Christian and Viking influences. Stave churches are among the oldest wooden buildings in the world.

Storting: the Norwegian parliament

tundra: a treeless region that is characteristic of Arctic or alpine regions. The subsoil remains permanently frozen, and only plants such as lichens, mosses, herbs, and dwarf shrubs can grow there.

British Broadcasting Company. *BBC News.* **N.d.**
< http://news.bbc.co.uk/> **(October 9, 2001).**
This website is an extensive international news source. It contains political and cultural news, as well as country profiles, and is updated regularly.

Cable News Network. *CNN.com Europe.* **2001.**
< http://europe.cnn.com/> **(October 9, 2001).**
This website is a news source on European countries, including political and cultural news. It is updated regularly.

Collins, Andrew, and Tania Inowlocki, eds. *Fodor's Norway.* **New York: Fodor's Travel Publications, 2000.**
This book is a travel guide that includes in-depth chapters on Norway's culture and the sights to see in its major cities and geographical regions.

The Economist. **2001.**
<http://www.economist.com> **(October 5, 2001).**
The website for *The Economist* magazine, this site provides extensive news coverage of the world's economies, including "country briefings" (profiles) of nations. It is updated regularly.

The Europa World Yearbook, 2000. **London: Europa Publications Limited, 2000.**
This is an annual publication that includes coverage of Norway's recent history, economy, and government, as well as providing a wealth of statistics on population, employment, trade, and more. A short directory of offices and organizations is also included.

Frey, Elke, Gerhard Lemmer, and Helga Rahe. *Norway.* **Munich: Nelles Verlag, 1999.**
This travel guide includes chapters on politics, economics, history, and culture.

Odin. **N.d.**
<http://odin.dep.no/odin/engelsk/index-b-n-a.html> **(October 9, 2001).**
This website provides an extensive and well-rounded look at Norway. It is produced by the Royal Norwegian Ministry of Foreign Affairs and includes articles on culture, news, and history, as well as a special kids' section.

"PRB 2001 World Population Data Sheet." *Population Reference Bureau (PRB).* **2001.**
<http://www.prb.org> **(October 5, 2001).**
This annual statistics sheet provides a wealth of population, demographic, and health statistics for Norway and almost all countries in the world.

Ryder, Simon, ed. *Insight Guide Norway.* **Singapore: Apa Publications, 1999.**
This is an in-depth travel guide. It includes chapters and features on Norwegian history, people, culture, politics, cities, and geography.

Statistical Yearbook of Norway. **2001.**
<http://www.ssb.no/english/yearbook> **(October 5, 2001).**
This website contains hundreds of tables of information about Norway, including social, political, and population statistics.

Swaney, Deanna. *Norway: Hiking, Biking, and Vikings*. Melbourne, Australia: Lonely Planet Publications, 1999.
This is an in-depth travel guide. It includes chapters on Norway's geography, politics, economics, history, and culture.

Turner, Barry, ed. *The Statesmen's Yearbook: The Politics, Cultures, and Economics of the World, 2001*. New York: Macmillan Press, 2000.
This annual publication provides concise information on Norway's history, climate, government, economy, and culture, including relevant statistics.

U.S. Department of State Bureau of Public Affairs. "Background Note: Norway." *U.S. Department of State*. 1999.
< http://www.state.gov/r/pa/bgn/index.cfm?docid=3421> (October 9, 2001).
This website page provides a general profile of Norway, produced by the U.S. Department of State. The profile includes brief summaries of the nation's geography, people, government and politics, and economy.

Washington Post. 2001.
<http://www.washingtonpost.com> (October 9, 2001).
This is the website for the *Washington Post* newspaper. It contains extensive international news coverage, including political and cultural stories about Norway.

The World Bank Group. 2001.
<http://www.worldbank.org> (October 9, 2001).
This website is a great resource for political and social statistics for Norway and nearly all countries in the world.

Asbjørnsen, Peter, and Jørgen Moe. *Norwegian Folk Tales: From the Collection of Peter Christen Asbjørnsen, Jørgen Moe.* New York: Pantheon Books, 1982.
This illustrated translation of Norwegian folktales features witches, trolls, ogres, sly foxes, mysterious bears, princesses, and country lads turned heroes.

Beach, Hugh. *A Year in Lapland: Guest of the Reindeer Herders.* Seattle, WA: University of Washington Press, 2001.
An American anthropologist recalls his first year among the Sami reindeer herders. This book is an homage to a threatened way of life.

Brundtland, Gro Harlem. *Madame Prime Minister: The Memoirs of the First Woman Leader of Norway.* New York: Farrar Straus & Giroux, 2002.
Dr. Gro Harlem Brundtland discusses her life and career.

Dahl, Hans Frederik. *Quisling: A Study in Treachery.* Translated by Anne-Marie Stanton-Ife. Abridged edition. New York: Cambridge University Press, 1999.
This biography of Quisling, whose name has become synonymous with "traitor," traces his career, through his trial and execution for high treason in 1945.

Gaarder, Jostein. *Sophie's World: A Novel about the History of Philosophy.* Translated by Paulette Moller. New York: Berkley Books, 1997.
This popular novel is about a young girl, Sophie, who becomes embroiled in a discussion of philosophy with a faceless correspondent. She also must unravel a mystery involving another young girl, Hilde, by using everything she's learning.

Holte, Elisabeth, and Sølvi Dos Santos. *Living in Norway.* Paris: Flammarion, 1993.
This full-color photobook gives a season-by-season look at life in Norway.

Ibsen, Henrik. *A Doll's House.* Adapted by Frank McGuinnes. New York: Dramatists Play Service, 1998.
This play is a critical view of a male-dominated and authoritarian society, presented with a realism that changed drama.

Larrington, Carolyne. *The Poetic Edda.* Oxford: Oxford University Press, 1999.
The *Poetic Edda* is the oldest known collection of Norwegian poems. It contains the great narratives of the creation of the world and the coming of Ragnarok, the Doom of the Gods.

Libæk, Ivar, and Øivind Stenersen. *A History of Norway from the Ice Age to the Age of Petroleum.* Translated by Jean Aase. Oslo: Grøndahl Dreyer, 1999.
This history of Norway, from the earliest known humans to the end of the twentieth century, includes an examination of Norway's expanding international role.

Norway.org
<http://www.norway.org>
This is the official website of the Royal Norwegian Embassy in the United

States. The site provides regularly updated news on politics, economy, culture, and education, as well as information on visiting and traveling in Norway.

The Norway Post
<http://www.norwaypost.no>
The *Norway Post* is a Norwegian newspaper in English. It provides international and domestic news.

Odin
<http://odin.dep.no/odin/engelsk/index-b-n-a.html>
This site provides extensive and well-rounded look at Norway, produced by the Royal Norwegian Ministry of Foreign Affairs. It includes articles on culture, news, history, and a special kids' section.

Orrell, Robert. *Blowout*. Dobbs Ferry, NY: Sheridan House, 2000.
This book is the memoir of a radio operator on the Hewett "A" drilling platform in the North Sea. Orrell recounts life on board the platform as well as a disastrous blowout and ensuing fire.

Robinson, Deborah B. *The Sami of Northern Europe*. Minneapolis, MN: Lerner Publications Company, 2002.
This book describes the history, modern and traditional cultural practices, and modern and traditional economies of the Sami, the indigenous people of Arctic Sweden, Norway, Finland, and Russia. It gives information about the geography and wildlife of the Arctic region and describes Sami religion, family life, language, and the arts.

Sawyer, Peter. *The Oxford Illustrated History of the Vikings*. Oxford: Oxford University Press, 1997.
This is a collection of illustrated essays about the history of the Vikings.

Simon, Charnan. *Leif Eriksson and the Vikings*. Chicago: Children's Press, 1991.
This book relates the adventures of the Norse explorer who left Greenland to sail west into uncharted waters in search of new land.

Undset, Sigrid. *Kristin Lavransdatter*. New York: Knopf, 1985.
Sigrid Undset won the Nobel Prize in 1928 for the three novels anthologized here—*The Bridal Wreath, The Mistress of Husaby,* and *The Cross.* This trilogy follows its title character through her life in fourteenth-century Scandinavia.

Valebrokk, Eva. *Norway's Stave Churches: Architecture, History, and Legends*. Translated by Ann Clay Zwick. Oslo: Boksenteret, 1997.
With many beautiful, full-color photos, this book describes the history and significance of stave churches in general and contains a separate chapter for each of the twenty-nine surviving stave churches.

vgsbooks.com
<http://www.vgsbooks.com>
Visit vgsbooks.com, the homepage of the Visual Geography Series®. You can get linked to all sorts of useful on-line information, including geographical, historical, demographic, cultural, and economic websites. The vgsbooks.com site is a great resource for late-breaking news and statistics.

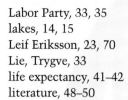

Labor Party, 33, 35
lakes, 14, 15
Leif Eriksson, 23, 70
Lie, Trygve, 33
life expectancy, 41–42
literature, 48–50

manufacturing, 60–61
maps, 7, 12
merchant marine, 29, 33, 59
Midnight Sun, Land of the, 9, 15
Midsummer Eve, 46
mountains, 10–11, 13
Mælstrom Current, 13

Napoleonic Wars, 28
National Insurance Act, 33
nationalism, 30, 49, 51–52
Nobel Prize, 50
Nordic Council, 33
Nord Norge (North Norway), 11–13, 38
North Atlantic Current, 14
North Atlantic Ocean, 4, 9, 17
North Atlantic Treaty Organization (NATO), 33
North Cape, 9
North Sea, 9, 34, 57
Norway: boundaries, size, and location, 8–9; currency, 68; flag, 69; independence, 5, 17, 30–31, 46; language, 48; maps, 7, 12; national anthem, 69; population, 4, 17–19, 22, 29, 38, 40; regions, 9–13
Norwegian Labor Party, 29
Norwegian Sea, 9, 57

oil, 5, 34, 35, 57–58
Oslo, 17–18
Olso, University of, 18

political parties, 29–30
pollution, 34

queens: Margaret, 27; Sonja, 35; Åsa, 23
Quisling, Vidkun, 32, 71

rainfall, 14–15
religion, 24, 25–26, 27, 44–45

rivers, 13–14
rosemaling, 51
royal family, 5, 36
Royal Norwegian Mint, 68
Russia, 9

Sami, 38–39
services, 58–60
shipping industry, 28, 61
Sigurdsson, Sverre, 26
Skagerrak, 9, 13
social welfare, 5–6, 29, 31, 33, 39, 40–41, 56–57, 64–65
sports and recreation, 6, 18, 54–55
standard of living, 5, 41, 56
Statoil, 58, 65
Stiklestad, Battle of, 25
Storting (Parliament), 28–30, 33, 35, 36–37
Sverdrup, Johan, 29
Svold, Battle of, 25
Sørlandet (South Country), 10–12

Thorvaldson, Erik (Erik the Red), 23
timber, 28, 63
topography, 9–13
tourism, 59
transportation system, 58–59
Treaty of Kiel, 28
Trondheim, 19
Trøndelag (Trondheim region), 11–13

United Nations (UN), 33, 64
United States, 29, 33

Venstre (Left) Party, 29
Vestlandet (West Country), 10–12
Vikings, 22–24, 48–49, 51
visual arts, 51–53
voting rights, 29–30, 36

whaling, 64
Winter Olympics, 54–55
World Health Organization, 35
World Heritage Site, 26, 72
World War I, 31
World War II, 19, 32–33

Østlandet (East Country), 10–12

Captions for photos appearing on cover and chapter openers:

Cover: The golden light of summer's midnight sun bathes Moskenesøya Island.

pp. 4–5 The fishing port Ålesund spreads across two islands connected by bridges.

pp. 8–9 The Lofoten Archipelago is a majestic, rocky landscape.

pp. 20–21 Norway's earliest inhabitants created these petroglyphs near Skjeberg.

pp. 38–39 In the annual Holsdagen Pageant in Hol, residents reenact a traditional wedding. The bridal party rides on horseback. Guests accompany them by horse-drawn carriage.

pp. 44–45 Sculptor Gustav Vigeland designed the architecture and landscape of Vigeland Park in Oslo as well as the 212 outdoor sculptures on display there.

Photo Acknowledgments
The images in this book are used with the permission of: © Wolfgang Kaehler, pp. 4–5, 15, 19 (top), 43, 60; © Trip/R. Belbin, pp. 6, 58; © Trip/N. Ray, pp. 8–9; © Trip/Eric Smith, p. 10; © Hans-Olaf Pfannkuch, pp. 13, 19 (bottom), 61, 63 (top); © Kirtley-Perkins/Visuals Unlimited, p. 16; © Fritz Pölking Visuals Unlimited, p. 17; © Blaine Harrington III, pp. 18, 44–45, 63 (bottom); © Liv Dahl, pp. 20–21, 37, 40, 53; © North Wind Pictures, pp. 22, 24, 49; Hulton Archive / Getty Images, pp. 25, 31, 32; © R. Al Simpson/Visuals Unlimited, p. 27; © Universitetetbiblioteket i Oslo, p. 28; © United Nations, p. 33; © AFP/CORBIS, p. 35 (both), 55; © Trip/N. & J. Wiseman, pp. 38–39; © SIU/Visuals Unlimited, p. 41; © Trip/G.V. Press, p. 46; © Norwegian Information Service, p. 50 (top and bottom); © Adam Woolfitt/CORBIS, p. 51; © National Gallery, Oslo, p. 52; © Trip/M. Barlow, p. 59; © Trip/P. Barker, p. 62; Todd Strand/IPS, p. 68; Laura Westlund, p. 69.

Cover photo: © John Noble/CORBIS. Back cover photo: NASA.